**Ask MrCareer**
*101 Common Questions About Careers and Their Answers*

## Welcome to:

## Ask MrCareer
### "101 Common Questions About Careers and Their Answers"

### By: Clarence E. Riley

"Your career isn't just a job; it's your journey toward purpose, growth, and fulfillment. Let's make every step count."

Copyright © 2025 Clarence Riley
All Rights Reserved

# Ask MrCareer
## *101 Common Questions About Careers and Their Answers*

Table of Contents

Introduction ................................................................................... 7
General Career Insights ................................................................. 9
   #01 - What is a career, and how is it different from a job? ............... 9
   #02 - Why do people need careers? ................................................ 10
   #03 - How does one's career define personal identity? ................... 11
   #04 - What is the meaning of "career fulfillment"? ......................... 12
   #05 - Why is having a career plan important? ................................ 13
   #06 - How can a career align with personal values? ....................... 14
   #07 - What are the benefits of long-term career planning? ............. 15
   #08 - What are the key differences between a traditional career path and a modern one? ................................................................. 16
   #09 - How has technology changed career opportunities? ............. 18
   #10 - Is it ever too late to start a new career? ................................. 19
Choosing a Career ......................................................................... 20
   #11 - How do I choose the right career for me? ............................. 20
   #12 - Should I follow my passion or the paycheck? ....................... 22
   #13 - How important is personality in career choice? .................... 23
   #14 - What role does education play in career success? ................ 24
   #15 - How can I match my skills with the right career? ................. 25
   #16 - Should I choose a career based on industry demand? .......... 27
   #17 - What are the best career options for introverts? .................. 28
   #18 - What are the best career options for extroverts? ................. 29
   #19 - How do I handle pressure from family when choosing a career? ........................................................................................... 30
   #20 - Can hobbies become successful careers? ............................. 33

# Ask MrCareer
## *101 Common Questions About Careers and Their Answers*

Career Advancement ................................................................ 37

   #21 - How do I get promoted in my current career? ................ 37

   #22 - What are the most important skills for career advancement? ................................................................................ 39

   #23 - How do I stand out in a competitive job market? ........... 41

   #24 - Should I go back to school to advance my career? ......... 42

   #25 - How do certifications impact career growth? ................. 43

   #26 - How important is networking for career advancement? ....... 44

   #27 - How do I handle rejection when trying to move up? ......... 45

   #28 - What is "imposter syndrome," and how can I overcome it? . 46

   #29 - Should I consider a lateral move for career growth? ....... 47

   #30 - How do I build a personal brand for my career? .............. 50

Career Changes ........................................................................ 54

   #31 - When is it time to change careers? ................................ 54

   #32 - How do I transition into a completely new industry? ....... 56

   #33 - What challenges come with starting over in a career? ..... 57

   #34 - How can I leverage transferable skills for a career change? .. 58

   #35 - How do I overcome fear when switching careers? ............ 60

   #36 - Is it better to be a specialist or a generalist? .................. 62

   #37 - How do I handle a career gap? ....................................... 63

   #38 - How do I explain a career change in an interview? ......... 64

   #39 - Should I change careers if I feel unfulfilled? ................... 65

   #40 - How do I prepare financially for a career shift? .............. 66

Working from Home and Remote Careers ............................... 67

   #41 - What are the advantages and challenges of working from home? ................................................................................... 67

# Ask MrCareer
## *101 Common Questions About Careers and Their Answers*

#42 - How do I stay productive in a remote career? ...... 69

#43 - How do I find legitimate work-from-home jobs? ................ 71

#44 - What skills are essential for remote work success? ............. 73

#45 - How can I maintain work-life balance while working remotely ........ 75

Entrepreneurship and Freelancing ........................ 77

#46 - Should I start my own business or stick to employment? ..... 77

#47 - What are the first steps to becoming an entrepreneur? ....... 79

#48 - How do I transition from a full-time job to freelancing? ....... 81

#49 - What challenges do freelancers face? ................. 83

#50 - How do I market myself as a freelancer? ................ 85

#51 - Is entrepreneurship a good career choice for everyone? ...... 87

#52 - How do I manage income uncertainty as a freelancer? ......... 89

#53 - How do I know if I'm ready to start my own business? ......... 90

#54 - What industries are best for entrepreneurs? ................ 91

#55 - How can I stay motivated as a self-employed professional? .. 93

Work-Life Balance and Career Satisfaction ........................ 95

#56 - How do I balance my career and personal life? ................. 95

#57 - What does "career satisfaction" mean? ................. 97

#58 - How do I avoid career burnout? ................ 98

#59 - Should I prioritize work or family when conflicts arise? ........ 99

#60 - How do I handle stress in high-pressure careers? ............. 100

Career and Education ........................ 101

#61 - Is a college degree necessary for a successful career? ........ 101

#62 - What are alternative career paths for those without degrees? ........ 102

# Ask MrCareer
## *101 Common Questions About Careers and Their Answers*

#63 - How do I choose the right major for my career goals?........103

#64 - How do I balance work and further education? ..................104

#65 - What role do internships play in launching a career?..........105

Challenges in Careers ...................................................................106

#66 - How do I handle a toxic work environment? .......................106

#67 - What should I do if I feel stuck in my career? .....................108

#68 - How do I deal with workplace discrimination......................110

#69 - How do I stay motivated in a stagnant job?........................112

#70 - How do I deal with being overqualified for jobs? ................113

Future of Work ..............................................................................114

#71 - What are the careers of the future? ...................................114

#72 - How will artificial intelligence impact job opportunities? ...116

#73 - What industries are on the rise?.........................................117

#74 - How do I future-proof my career? ......................................118

#75 - What is the gig economy, and how does it affect careers?..119

Specialized Careers........................................................................120

#76 - What are the best careers in STEM? ...................................120

#77 - What are the highest-paying careers without a degree?.....122

#78 - How do I enter creative industries like art or writing?.........124

#79 - How can I succeed in healthcare careers? ..........................126

#80 - What are career options for veterans? ...............................128

Soft Skills and Career Success .......................................................130

#81 - Why are communication skills critical for career success?..130

#82 - How do I develop leadership skills? ....................................132

# Ask MrCareer
## *101 Common Questions About Careers and Their Answers*

#83 - What are the most valuable interpersonal skills for the workplace? ................................................................. 133

#84 - How do I handle conflict in the workplace? ...................... 134

#85 - How do I build confidence in my abilities? ..................... 135

Miscellaneous Topics ........................................................ 136

#86 - What are the best tools for career planning? ................. 136

#87 - How do I write an effective resume? ............................. 138

#88 - What is the importance of mentorship in a career? ........... 140

#89 - How do internships help in career building? .................. 141

#90 - Should I work abroad to grow my career? ...................... 142

Job Search and Interviews .................................................. 143

#91 - How do I prepare for an interview? .............................. 143

#92 - What are the best ways to find a job? .......................... 145

#93 - How do I negotiate my salary? ................................... 146

#94 - What questions should I ask in an interview? ................ 147

#95 - How do I deal with job rejections? ............................. 148

Retirement and Legacy ....................................................... 149

#96 - How do I plan for retirement in my career? ................... 149

#97 - What is the legacy I want to leave in my career? ........... 151

#98 - How do I stay active after retiring from my career? ....... 153

#99 - What are second-act careers? ..................................... 155

#100 - How do I pass on career wisdom to the next generation? 157

Final Question ............................................................... 158

#101 - How do I define success in my career? ....................... 158

Final Thoughts ................................................................ 159

# Ask MrCareer
## *101 Common Questions About Careers and Their Answers*

Notes .......................................................................................... 161

# Ask MrCareer
## *101 Common Questions About Careers and Their Answers*

## Introduction

Navigating the world of careers can feel overwhelming, no matter where you are in your professional journey. Whether you're a recent graduate seeking direction, a seasoned professional considering a career change, or someone striving to advance in your current role, the road to achieving your career goals is often filled with questions, decisions, and uncertainties. That's where *Ask MrCareer* comes in.

This book is designed to serve as a comprehensive guide to the most common career-related questions people face. Drawing on years of experience in career guidance and professional development, *Ask MrCareer* provides practical, thoughtful, and actionable answers to help you make informed decisions at every stage of your career. Each question has been carefully curated to address real-world concerns, covering topics such as choosing the right career, advancing in your field, handling setbacks, leveraging your skills, and even turning hobbies into fulfilling work.

What sets this book apart is its accessibility and relevance. The answers are crafted to provide not only clarity but also encouragement, empowering you to take charge of your professional life. Whether you're pondering whether to follow your passion or a paycheck, wondering if it's too late to start a new career, or seeking advice on standing out in a competitive job market, the insights here are tailored to meet you where you are.

The book is organized to ensure that readers can quickly find answers to their pressing questions, while also gaining a holistic understanding of the broader career landscape. From foundational topics like understanding what defines a career to advanced strategies like building a personal brand, the answers

# Ask MrCareer
## *101 Common Questions About Careers and Their Answers*

aim to equip you with the knowledge and confidence to take the next step forward.

*Ask MrCareer* doesn't just provide answers; it encourages reflection and self-discovery. Careers are deeply personal and often intertwined with our identities, values, and aspirations. This book invites you to think critically about your goals, align your choices with your values, and embrace opportunities for growth and reinvention.

Whether you're looking to secure your first job, break into a new industry, or redefine your professional path, *Ask MrCareer* is here to guide you. The questions and answers serve as a toolkit to help you overcome challenges, maximize opportunities, and achieve a fulfilling career.

Your career journey is unique, and this book is designed to support you every step of the way. With practical advice, thoughtful insights, and encouragement to take bold steps, *Ask MrCareer* is more than a resource—it's your companion in building the career you deserve.

# Ask MrCareer
## *101 Common Questions About Careers and Their Answers*

## General Career Insights

### #01 - What is a career, and how is it different from a job?

A career is a long-term journey that encompasses a series of roles, experiences, and achievements within a particular field or industry. It reflects an individual's professional growth and commitment to a chosen path, often evolving through deliberate planning, skill acquisition, and goal setting. Careers are about progression and development, focusing on building expertise, reputation, and personal fulfillment over time.

In contrast, a job is a specific position or task performed within an organization to earn income. Jobs are often temporary or transactional, focusing on fulfilling immediate needs such as paying bills or gaining work experience. While a career is broader and more strategic, a job is often a stepping stone within the larger career framework.

For example, a person working as a teacher might consider their job the daily responsibilities they undertake, such as lesson planning or grading. However, their career includes their overall progression in education, such as earning advanced degrees, mentoring other teachers, or becoming a school administrator.

The distinction lies in purpose and scope: a job is about the present, while a career is about the future. Careers often involve continuous learning and adapting to changing goals, while jobs can be singular, short-term engagements. While all careers are made up of jobs, not all jobs lead to a career.

# Ask MrCareer
## *101 Common Questions About Careers and Their Answers*

## #02 - Why do people need careers?

People need careers for several reasons:

- **Financial Stability**: A career offers the opportunity for long-term financial security through consistent income and career advancement.

- **Personal Growth**: Careers provide a framework for developing skills, achieving goals, and growing professionally.

- **Purpose and Fulfillment**: A career can provide a sense of purpose, allowing people to contribute meaningfully to society, their communities, or specific causes.

- **Social Identity**: Careers often play a significant role in how individuals are perceived by others and how they view themselves. Many people derive their sense of identity from their work.

- **Stability and Direction**: A well-defined career path offers a sense of stability and direction in life, helping individuals plan for the future.

# Ask MrCareer
## *101 Common Questions About Careers and Their Answers*

## #03 - How does one's career define personal identity?

One's career is often deeply tied to personal identity because it reflects a person's values, passions, and aspirations. The work we do often shapes how we see ourselves and how we are perceived by others. A person's career choices can convey information about their interests, skills, and even their social status. Many people feel a strong sense of pride in their careers because the work they do aligns with their personal values and goals. Additionally, professional success or challenges can influence self-esteem and how a person feels about their contributions to the world.

A career can become a core part of a person's identity, influencing their relationships, lifestyle, and even personal priorities.

# Ask MrCareer
## 101 Common Questions About Careers and Their Answers

## #04 - What is the meaning of "career fulfillment"?

Career fulfillment refers to the sense of satisfaction and contentment that comes from doing meaningful and rewarding work. It involves a combination of factors such as achieving professional goals, feeling valued at work, using one's skills to their fullest potential, and aligning one's work with personal values. Career fulfillment is not only about salary or promotion but also about the work environment, the impact of one's contributions, and the overall balance between work and personal life. When someone feels fulfilled in their career, they are often motivated, engaged, and have a deeper sense of purpose in their work.

# Ask MrCareer
## *101 Common Questions About Careers and Their Answers*

## #05 - Why is having a career plan important?

Having a **career plan** is important because it provides direction and helps individuals take proactive steps toward achieving their professional goals. It allows for:

- **Clear Goals**: Setting specific career objectives helps to maintain focus and measure progress.

- **Career Development**: A plan helps individuals develop necessary skills and seek opportunities for growth and advancement.

- **Informed Decision Making**: A career plan allows individuals to make informed choices about jobs, education, and career opportunities that align with long-term goals.

- **Motivation**: With a clear path in mind, individuals are more likely to stay motivated and driven to overcome obstacles.

- **Work-Life Balance**: Planning a career also helps in considering how to balance professional demands with personal life.

A well-thought-out career plan helps individuals remain focused and adaptable, even when faced with challenges or changes in the job market.

# Ask MrCareer
## *101 Common Questions About Careers and Their Answers*

# #06 - How can a career align with personal values?

A career can align with personal values by ensuring that the work you do and the organization you work for reflect what is most important to you. This alignment involves:

- **Choosing the Right Field**: Selecting a career path in an industry or profession that matches your passions, whether it's helping others, working with technology, or contributing to environmental sustainability.

- **Workplace Culture**: Finding a company whose culture, mission, and goals align with your personal beliefs and ethics. For example, if integrity is a key value for you, working for an organization that prioritizes ethical practices may provide greater job satisfaction.

- **Meaningful Work**: Engaging in roles or projects that contribute to causes or goals that you believe in, such as social impact work, healthcare, education, or arts and culture.

- **Decision Making**: Continuously evaluating career decisions through the lens of personal values, ensuring that work-life balance, family commitments, and job satisfaction remain in harmony with individual priorities.

When your career aligns with your personal values, it can lead to greater fulfillment and a deeper connection to your work.

# Ask MrCareer
## *101 Common Questions About Careers and Their Answers*

# #07 - What are the benefits of long-term career planning?

The benefits of long-term career planning include:

- **Clear Direction**: A long-term plan helps you define career objectives, milestones, and timelines, allowing you to stay focused and on track.

- **Personal Growth**: Planning for the long term ensures that you continue to develop your skills and knowledge, advancing in your chosen field.

- **Adaptability**: Long-term planning enables you to anticipate industry trends and changes, allowing you to adapt and remain competitive in the job market.

- **Job Satisfaction**: A well-planned career allows you to pursue roles that align with your interests and values, leading to greater fulfillment in the workplace.

- **Career Security**: With a long-term plan, you are more likely to make strategic decisions that increase job security, financial stability, and overall career satisfaction.

By planning ahead, individuals can avoid career stagnation and ensure that they are always progressing toward their ultimate professional goals.

# Ask MrCareer
*101 Common Questions About Careers and Their Answers*

# #08 - What are the key differences between a traditional career path and a modern one?

Key differences between a **traditional career path** and a **modern career path** include:

- **Job Stability**: In traditional careers, employees often stayed with one company or in the same profession for a lifetime. Modern careers, however, often involve more frequent job changes and career shifts, with people moving between different roles, industries, or even starting their own businesses.

- **Career Progression**: Traditional careers tend to follow a linear progression, with employees advancing up the corporate ladder in a set sequence. Modern careers, however, are often more flexible, with lateral moves, project-based roles, and unconventional career paths being more common.

- **Workplace Environment**: Traditional careers were often characterized by rigid office hours and centralized office spaces. Today, modern careers feature remote work, flexible hours, and more decentralized, tech-driven work environments.

- **Learning and Growth**: In the past, career advancement was often linked to formal education and internal training programs. Today, professionals are more likely to upskill through online courses, certifications, and informal learning.

- **Technology Integration**: Traditional careers may not have embraced technological changes as quickly. Modern careers, on the other hand, frequently

# Ask MrCareer
## *101 Common Questions About Careers and Their Answers*

incorporate new technologies, creating opportunities for people to work remotely or in tech-driven fields.

# Ask MrCareer
## 101 Common Questions About Careers and Their Answers

# #09 - How has technology changed career opportunities?

Technology has drastically transformed career opportunities by:

- **Remote Work**: Technology allows people to work from anywhere, opening up global job markets and offering flexibility in working hours.

- **Automation and AI**: Advances in automation and AI have created new job opportunities in tech fields and have transformed traditional roles by streamlining tasks or replacing certain jobs.

- **Online Learning and Certifications**: The internet has made education more accessible, allowing individuals to learn new skills and pursue certifications without attending traditional universities.

- **Gig Economy**: Technology has fostered the rise of freelancing, contracting, and part-time work, leading to the gig economy where people can take on short-term roles or create their own businesses.

- **Job Market Expansion**: Technology has led to the growth of entirely new industries such as cybersecurity, data science, and digital marketing, creating new career paths that didn't exist a few decades ago.

The rapid pace of technological advancement means that people need to adapt and continuously upskill to remain competitive in the job market.

# Ask MrCareer
## *101 Common Questions About Careers and Their Answers*

## #10 - Is it ever too late to start a new career?

No, it is never too late to start a new career. Many people successfully transition into new fields later in life by:

- **Leveraging Existing Skills**: Even if you're changing careers, you may have transferable skills, such as leadership, communication, or problem-solving, that can be valuable in a new role.

- **Continuous Learning**: With online courses, certifications, and training programs, individuals can acquire new skills and knowledge that allow them to pursue a new career, regardless of age.

- **Networking**: A strong network can help open doors in a new field. People often leverage their existing connections to transition into new industries.

- **Mentorship**: Mentors in a new field can provide guidance, insights, and encouragement, helping to smooth the transition.

- **Increased Life Experience**: Later in life, people may have a clearer sense of their passions and strengths, which can make a career change more meaningful and fulfilling.

Changing careers at any age can be a fulfilling and rewarding experience, as long as the individual is committed to learning and adapting to new opportunities.

# Ask MrCareer
## *101 Common Questions About Careers and Their Answers*

# Choosing a Career

## #11 - How do I choose the right career for me?

Choosing the right career involves a combination of self-awareness, research, and planning. To find a career that aligns with your strengths, interests, and values, consider the following steps:

- **Assess Your Interests**: Think about the activities and subjects that naturally engage you. Reflect on what you enjoy doing in your free time, whether it's working with people, solving problems, being creative, or working with your hands.

- **Evaluate Your Strengths and Skills**: Identify your natural talents and areas where you excel. Consider taking a skills assessment or career aptitude test to gain more clarity on potential fields that align with your abilities.

- **Align with Your Values**: Choose a career that reflects your personal values and priorities. Whether it's a desire for work-life balance, job stability, helping others, or earning a high salary, make sure the career you pursue is aligned with your long-term goals.

- **Research Career Options**: Explore different fields by reading about them, speaking with professionals in those areas, or shadowing someone in your desired field. This helps you understand the realities of different careers.

- **Consider Job Prospects**: Look into the demand for specific roles in the job market, salary expectations, and future career growth. Make sure there are opportunities for advancement in the path you choose.

# Ask MrCareer
## *101 Common Questions About Careers and Their Answers*

- **Seek Guidance**: Speak with mentors, career coaches, or professionals in your desired field to get advice and insights.

The right career is one that balances your passions, skills, and market demand while offering room for personal and professional growth.

# Ask MrCareer
### *101 Common Questions About Careers and Their Answers*

## #12 - Should I follow my passion or the paycheck?

This question often arises when you're unsure whether to choose a career based on what you love or a job that offers financial stability. Ideally, your career should offer a balance of both, but here's how to approach the decision:

- **Following Your Passion**: Choosing a career based on your passion can bring deep fulfillment and motivation. If you truly love what you do, you are likely to be more engaged, persistent, and happier in your work. However, pursuing passion alone might not always lead to financial security, especially in competitive or niche fields.

- **Following the Paycheck**: If your primary concern is financial stability, a high-paying job might seem appealing. However, jobs purely driven by monetary compensation can lead to burnout and dissatisfaction if you're not passionate about the work. Job security and a steady income are crucial, but they may not provide long-term fulfillment if the work doesn't align with your interests.

The best approach is often to find a compromise where your work aligns with your values and interests, while also providing adequate compensation and job stability. It's important to strike a balance between doing something you love and meeting your financial needs.

# Ask MrCareer
## *101 Common Questions About Careers and Their Answers*

## #13 - How important is personality in career choice?

Your personality plays a significant role in determining the right career for you, as it influences how you interact with others, manage stress, and approach tasks. Here's why personality matters:

- **Work Environment Fit**: Some careers may require specific traits that align with the work environment. For example, extroverts may thrive in social or customer-facing roles, while introverts might prefer jobs that allow them to work independently or in smaller groups.

- **Job Suitability**: Your personality affects how well you'll enjoy and succeed in particular jobs. For instance, someone who is detail-oriented and enjoys structure may do well in accounting or engineering, while a creative person might excel in marketing or design.

- **Stress Management**: Some jobs involve high pressure or uncertainty, requiring individuals with resilient personalities who can handle stress. Others, like administrative roles, may require a calm and organized demeanor.

- **Team Dynamics**: Understanding your personality can help you choose whether to work in a collaborative team or prefer working individually. Some people thrive in team-based environments, while others perform best when working solo.

Personality assessments, such as the Myers-Briggs Type Indicator (MBTI) or the Holland Code, can be helpful tools in identifying careers that align with your personality traits.

# Ask MrCareer
*101 Common Questions About Careers and Their Answers*

## #14 - What role does education play in career success?

Education plays a significant role in shaping career opportunities, but its importance varies depending on the field:

- **Foundational Knowledge**: Formal education provides foundational knowledge and critical thinking skills necessary for many careers, especially in fields like healthcare, engineering, finance, and law.
- **Skills Development**: Education helps individuals develop specific technical or professional skills, whether through a degree, vocational training, or certifications.
- **Networking**: Educational institutions often provide valuable networking opportunities, connecting students with peers, professors, and professionals in their chosen field.
- **Credentialing**: Many careers require certain educational qualifications or certifications. For example, becoming a doctor, lawyer, or teacher requires extensive education and training.
- **Career Flexibility**: Higher education can also provide the flexibility to switch careers or advance in a profession by expanding your skill set.

However, education is not the only factor determining career success. Experience, interpersonal skills, and a strong work ethic also play critical roles. In some cases, self-directed learning, on-the-job experience, and professional certifications can be just as valuable as formal education.

# Ask MrCareer
## *101 Common Questions About Careers and Their Answers*

# #15 - How can I match my skills with the right career?

Matching your skills with the right career involves identifying your strengths and interests, then finding roles that make the most of them:

- **Assess Your Skills**: List your hard and soft skills. Hard skills are technical abilities or knowledge specific to certain tasks (e.g., coding, accounting), while soft skills include communication, leadership, and problem-solving.

- **Consider Interests and Strengths**: Evaluate what you naturally excel at and what you enjoy doing. If you're good at organizing and planning, a career in project management may be ideal. If you're creative and love working with people, marketing, design, or communications could be a good fit.

- **Explore Career Options**: Use career assessments or speak to mentors to explore careers that value your skill set. Many online platforms and career counseling services offer tools to match skills with potential career paths.

- **Gain Experience**: Internships, volunteer work, and freelance opportunities can give you the chance to test different careers, refine your skills, and build experience in a field of interest.

- **Continuous Learning**: If your current skills don't match the career you want, consider taking courses, earning certifications, or gaining experience to bridge the gap.

# Ask MrCareer
## *101 Common Questions About Careers and Their Answers*

By identifying your skills and seeking opportunities that align with them, you'll increase your chances of finding a fulfilling and successful career.

# Ask MrCareer
## *101 Common Questions About Careers and Their Answers*

# #16 - Should I choose a career based on industry demand?

Choosing a career based on industry demand can be a smart strategy, especially if you're looking for job security and opportunities for growth. Here's why:

- **Job Security**: Industries experiencing growth typically offer more job opportunities and greater job security. For example, technology, healthcare, and renewable energy sectors are expected to grow substantially in the coming years.

- **Increased Earnings Potential**: High-demand industries often offer higher salaries due to competition for talent and the need for specialized skills.

- **Opportunities for Advancement**: Growing industries often have more opportunities for advancement, allowing you to move up the career ladder more quickly.

- **Market Trends**: By analyzing market trends, you can predict which fields will thrive, giving you a competitive edge in choosing the right career.

However, it's also important to choose a career that aligns with your interests and values. While industry demand can be a factor, long-term career satisfaction often comes from doing work you find meaningful and engaging.

# Ask MrCareer
## *101 Common Questions About Careers and Their Answers*

# #17- What are the best career options for introverts?

Introverts tend to thrive in careers that allow for independent work, minimal social interaction, or work in smaller teams. Here are some great career options for introverts:

- **Writing and Editing**: Careers in journalism, copywriting, or content creation allow introverts to express themselves through writing, with minimal face-to-face interaction.

- **Research and Analysis**: Roles such as data analysis, scientific research, or market research suit introverts who prefer working with information and solving problems.

- **Design and Technology**: Careers in graphic design, web development, and software engineering allow introverts to work independently or in small teams while utilizing their technical skills.

- **Accounting and Finance**: These fields often require individual work and attention to detail, with limited social interaction.

- **Healthcare**: While some healthcare careers require direct patient interaction, roles such as medical laboratory technician, medical coder, or radiologist may involve more solo work.

Introverts often excel in careers that require focus, concentration, and the ability to work independently.

# Ask MrCareer
## *101 Common Questions About Careers and Their Answers*

## #18 - What are the best career options for extroverts?

Extroverts thrive in careers that involve social interaction, teamwork, and active engagement with others. Here are some great career options for extroverts:

- **Sales and Marketing**: Extroverts often excel in sales, advertising, and public relations, where they can interact with clients, network, and promote products or services.

- **Public Relations and Media**: Careers in media, communications, and public relations allow extroverts to work with the public and represent brands or individuals.

- **Education and Training**: Teaching, coaching, or training roles are ideal for extroverts who enjoy engaging with people and sharing knowledge.

- **Event Planning**: This field involves organizing events, managing logistics, and working closely with clients, which suits extroverts who are social and detail-oriented.

- **Healthcare**: Extroverts may enjoy roles like nursing, physical therapy, or medical sales, where they can work closely with patients and healthcare professionals.

Careers that involve interacting with others and facilitating teamwork are often best suited for extroverts, as they thrive in dynamic, people-focused environments.

# Ask MrCareer
*101 Common Questions About Careers and Their Answers*

# #19 - How do I handle pressure from family when choosing a career?

Handling pressure from family when choosing a career can be challenging, especially if their expectations conflict with your interests and aspirations. However, it is important to make decisions that align with your values, goals, and passions, rather than solely trying to meet family expectations. Here are steps to manage that pressure:

### 1. Communicate Openly

- **Express Your Feelings**: Start by having an honest and open conversation with your family about your career goals. Explain why you are choosing a particular path and how it aligns with your interests, strengths, and long-term goals.
- **Listen to Their Concerns**: Understand that your family might have your best interests at heart, and they may be concerned about your financial stability, job security, or happiness. Listening to their perspective can help you address their concerns thoughtfully.

### 2. Clarify Your Values and Goals

- **Know Your Priorities**: Reflect on what matters most to you in a career—whether it's passion, financial stability, work-life balance, or job satisfaction. This clarity will help you confidently explain your choices to others.
- **Set Personal Boundaries**: While family input is valuable, it's essential to maintain boundaries and make decisions that reflect your own ambitions. It's your career and future, and you are the one who will live with the consequences.

# Ask MrCareer
## *101 Common Questions About Careers and Their Answers*

### 3. Provide Evidence

- **Show Your Research**: If your family is concerned about the viability of your chosen career, show them that you've done thorough research. Present data on job market trends, salary potential, and success stories within your chosen field. Demonstrating that you've thought your decision through can alleviate some concerns.

- **Highlight Your Passion**: Sometimes, family may not understand why you're passionate about a particular career, especially if it's unconventional. Sharing your enthusiasm and explaining why it excites you can help them see that you are committed to your success.

### 4. Compromise and Be Flexible

- **Find a Middle Ground**: If your family is particularly insistent on a career path they believe is more secure or prestigious, consider finding a compromise. For example, pursuing a career that you're passionate about while also gaining transferable skills in areas they value may allow you to satisfy both your interests and their concerns.

- **Short-Term Solutions**: If the pressure is overwhelming, you could explore a career that offers some stability in the short term while transitioning to your dream job in the long term. This gives you time to prove your ability to succeed and ease family worries.

### 5. Seek Support from Other Mentors

- **Broaden Your Support System**: If your family is unsupportive, seek guidance and encouragement from other trusted individuals like mentors, friends, or colleagues who understand your goals. Sometimes, an external perspective can provide the confidence you need.

# Ask MrCareer
## *101 Common Questions About Careers and Their Answers*

- **Build Your Confidence**: The more confident and knowledgeable you are about your career choice, the less likely you are to be swayed by external pressure. Take time to learn and grow in your field, and your confidence will help you stand firm in your decision.

### 6. Be Patient

- **Give It Time**: Your family may not immediately understand or approve of your decision, but as you begin to succeed in your chosen career, they may start to see the value in it. Keep working toward your goals, and over time, the pressure from family may ease.

Ultimately, it's your career and your life. While it's important to consider your family's input, making decisions based on your own passions, goals, and strengths is key to long-term fulfillment and success.

# Ask MrCareer
## *101 Common Questions About Careers and Their Answers*

# #20- Can hobbies become successful careers?

Yes, hobbies can definitely evolve into successful careers, and many people have turned their passions into profitable ventures. However, turning a hobby into a career requires a mix of strategy, hard work, and sometimes a bit of risk-taking. Here's how you can make that transition:

**1. Evaluate the Viability of Your Hobby**

- **Passion vs. Market Demand**: The first step is to assess whether there's a market for your hobby. Is there demand for the product or service you provide, or is it something others might also find valuable? For example, turning a passion for photography into a career as a professional photographer can be viable if there's a demand for your style and expertise.

- **Identify Your Strengths**: Understand what aspects of your hobby you excel at and how they could translate into a marketable skill. If you love writing, for example, you might be able to turn that hobby into a career as a freelance writer, editor, or content creator.

**2. Develop Your Skill Set**

- **Refine Your Craft**: While hobbies are often based on personal enjoyment, turning them into a career requires mastery and expertise. Take courses, attend workshops, or seek mentorship to improve your skills and increase your chances of success.

- **Practice Consistently**: Just as professionals hone their skills over time, you must be committed to consistently practicing and improving in your chosen hobby. The more skilled and confident you become, the easier it will be to monetize it.

# Ask MrCareer
## *101 Common Questions About Careers and Their Answers*

### 3. Build a Brand or Reputation

- **Create an Online Presence**: If your hobby has the potential to become a career, building an online presence can help you reach a larger audience. For example, blogging about your hobby, sharing your projects on social media, or creating a YouTube channel can help you build a following.

- **Showcase Your Work**: Create a portfolio or showcase your work in a way that appeals to potential clients or customers. For example, if your hobby is crafting, you can create an online store or display your products on Etsy to start selling.

### 4. Monetize Your Hobby

- **Offer Services or Products**: Once you have honed your skills and established a presence, consider different ways to monetize your hobby. For instance, if you love cooking, you could start a catering business, offer cooking classes, or create a recipe blog.

- **Freelancing and Contract Work**: Many hobbies, like photography, graphic design, or writing, can be monetized by offering your services as a freelancer or contractor. By building a portfolio, networking, and reaching out to clients, you can transform a hobby into a full-time career.

- **Teaching and Mentorship**: If you are highly skilled in your hobby, consider offering courses or tutoring others. Whether it's teaching music lessons, giving art classes, or mentoring people interested in photography, there's often a market for knowledge and expertise.

# Ask MrCareer
## *101 Common Questions About Careers and Their Answers*

### 5. Create a Business Model

- **Understand the Financials**: Turning a hobby into a career involves learning the business side of things. This might include developing a pricing structure, creating a business plan, and learning how to manage expenses and profits.

- **Explore Multiple Income Streams**: Think about how you can diversify your income related to your hobby. For instance, if you love knitting, you might sell products, offer knitting tutorials, and even write a knitting book.

- **Set Long-Term Goals**: Like any business, turning a hobby into a career involves strategic planning. Set long-term goals for growth, scalability, and sustainability. You may need to invest in equipment, marketing, and other resources to make the transition successful.

### 6. Transition Gradually

- **Start Part-Time**: If you're unsure about making your hobby your full-time job right away, start by pursuing it part-time. For example, you might begin freelancing in your free time while still working a regular job. This allows you to build your portfolio and clientele without the risk of giving up your primary income too soon.

- **Build a Buffer**: Before making the leap, consider building a financial cushion to support you as you transition into your new career. This could include savings or keeping a part-time job while you grow your business.

### 7. Be Patient and Persistent

- **Expect Setbacks**: Like any career, turning a hobby into a full-time job takes time, persistence, and overcoming setbacks. There will be challenges, especially in the early

# Ask MrCareer
## *101 Common Questions About Careers and Their Answers*

stages, but staying focused on your passion and long-term goals will help you push through.

- **Adapt and Evolve**: As you grow in your new career, be open to adapting and evolving based on feedback and changing market demands. Flexibility is key to long-term success.

**Real-Life Examples**

Many people have successfully turned their hobbies into thriving careers. For example:

- **Photography**: A hobbyist photographer can turn their passion into a career by offering professional photography services for events, portraits, or commercial purposes.
- **Writing**: A hobby writer can publish books, freelance for magazines, or start a blog that generates income through ads or sponsored content.
- **Gaming**: Video game enthusiasts have turned their hobby into a career by streaming on platforms like Twitch, creating YouTube content, or becoming professional gamers.

**Conclusion**

Yes, hobbies can absolutely become successful careers with the right combination of skill development, market demand, and business acumen. However, making that transition requires dedication, patience, and a strategic approach to turning your passion into a professional pursuit. Whether it's through freelancing, teaching, or creating products, there are plenty of ways to make a living from something you love.

# Ask MrCareer
*101 Common Questions About Careers and Their Answers*

## Career Advancement

### #21 - How do I get promoted in my current career?

Getting promoted in your current career involves demonstrating your value, taking initiative, and positioning yourself as a key contributor. Here's how to increase your chances of promotion:

- **Excel in Your Current Role**: Consistently exceed expectations in your current responsibilities. Take the time to understand what is expected of you, then go above and beyond.

- **Show Leadership**: Even if you're not in a managerial position, demonstrate leadership qualities by taking initiative, helping colleagues, and driving projects forward.

- **Seek Opportunities for Growth**: Volunteer for high-impact projects that align with the company's goals and show your ability to handle more responsibility.

- **Develop New Skills**: Take on new challenges, acquire skills that are valuable for the next level, and show that you can handle more complex tasks.

- **Build Relationships with Leadership**: Network with decision-makers and senior leaders. Demonstrate your ambition and ask for feedback on how to improve your chances for advancement.

- **Have Career Conversations**: Discuss your career goals with your manager. Make it clear that you are interested in growth opportunities and ask for guidance on what steps to take to advance.

# Ask MrCareer
## *101 Common Questions About Careers and Their Answers*

By proving that you're ready for the next level and consistently delivering results, you position yourself as a strong candidate for promotion.

# Ask MrCareer
*101 Common Questions About Careers and Their Answers*

# #22 - What are the most important skills for career advancement?

The skills required for career advancement vary by industry and role, but here are some universally important skills:

- **Leadership and Management**: Being able to lead teams, manage projects, and make decisions is crucial for climbing the corporate ladder.

- **Communication**: Both verbal and written communication skills are essential, as they enable you to convey ideas clearly and build relationships.

- **Problem-Solving**: The ability to identify issues and create solutions is highly valued in every field. Employers look for individuals who can navigate challenges effectively.

- **Adaptability**: In today's rapidly changing job market, being able to adjust to new roles, technologies, and ways of working is key to long-term success.

- **Networking**: Building and maintaining a professional network can open up new opportunities for growth.

- **Emotional Intelligence**: Understanding your own emotions and those of others allows you to work effectively with colleagues and handle workplace challenges with professionalism.

- **Continuous Learning**: Being open to learning new skills, whether through formal education, certifications, or self-study, shows your commitment to personal and professional growth.

# Ask MrCareer
## *101 Common Questions About Careers and Their Answers*

By honing these skills, you can improve your career prospects and increase your chances of advancement.

# Ask MrCareer
## *101 Common Questions About Careers and Their Answers*

## #23 - How do I stand out in a competitive job market?

To stand out in a competitive job market, you need to showcase your unique skills, experience, and personality. Here's how:

- **Personal Branding**: Develop a personal brand that highlights your strengths and expertise. Create a professional online presence through platforms like LinkedIn, where you can showcase your experience and achievements.

- **Networking**: Build a strong network of professionals in your industry. Attend industry events, join professional organizations, and connect with others on LinkedIn.

- **Tailored Resume and Cover Letter**: Customize your resume and cover letter for each job you apply to, emphasizing the skills and experiences that align with the specific job requirements.

- **Upskill and Reskill**: Take courses or certifications to develop in-demand skills, particularly in areas like technology, project management, or leadership.

- **Show Results**: Highlight measurable achievements in your previous roles. Quantify how you contributed to the success of projects or improved business outcomes.

- **Interview Skills**: Practice answering common interview questions and tailor your responses to demonstrate how you are uniquely qualified for the role. Be prepared to explain how you can add value to the company.

By focusing on what makes you unique and continuously improving your skills, you can differentiate yourself from other candidates in a competitive job market.

# Ask MrCareer
## *101 Common Questions About Careers and Their Answers*

# #24 - Should I go back to school to advance my career?

Whether or not you should go back to school to advance your career depends on several factors:

- **Industry Requirements**: Some industries require advanced degrees or specialized certifications for career advancement (e.g., medicine, law, academia). In these cases, going back to school may be necessary.

- **Desired Role**: If your career goals require a higher level of expertise or a specific skill set, further education could open up new opportunities.

- **Cost vs. Benefit**: Evaluate whether the cost of tuition and the time commitment are justified by the potential career advancement and salary increase. Consider the return on investment.

- **Alternatives**: Sometimes, certifications, online courses, or boot camps are more affordable and faster ways to gain the skills you need to advance. These options can also be tailored to your specific career interests.

- **Work Experience**: Depending on your current job and field, hands-on experience may be more valuable than additional formal education. Some industries value practical experience over academic credentials.

If you're uncertain, talk to mentors or industry professionals to get their perspective on whether further education would help you reach your career goals.

# Ask MrCareer
## *101 Common Questions About Careers and Their Answers*

## #25 - How do certifications impact career growth?

Certifications can have a significant impact on career growth by demonstrating your expertise, enhancing your skill set, and making you more competitive in the job market:

- **Skill Validation**: Certifications validate your knowledge in a particular field or skill, showing employers that you have specialized knowledge or have mastered a specific area.

- **Increased Job Opportunities**: Many employers look for candidates with relevant certifications, especially in fields like IT, healthcare, project management, and finance. A certification can make you more attractive to employers.

- **Higher Earning Potential**: Certified professionals often earn higher salaries compared to their non-certified counterparts because certifications can indicate a higher level of competence.

- **Career Mobility**: Certifications can open doors for lateral moves or promotions, enabling you to switch to a different role or take on more responsibility.

- **Industry Credibility**: Being certified in your field can improve your credibility with clients, peers, and employers, demonstrating your commitment to ongoing professional development.

Before pursuing a certification, research which credentials are most respected in your industry and align with your career goals.

# Ask MrCareer
*101 Common Questions About Careers and Their Answers*

# #26 - How important is networking for career advancement?

Networking is one of the most important factors for career advancement. Here's why:

- **Access to Opportunities**: Networking helps you learn about job openings and career opportunities that may not be publicly advertised. Many positions are filled through referrals from professional connections.

- **Knowledge Sharing**: Building relationships with industry peers allows you to share insights, advice, and best practices. Networking helps you stay updated on trends and developments in your field.

- **Mentorship**: Networking provides opportunities to find mentors who can guide you in your career, offering advice and support as you navigate challenges and seek advancement.

- **Increased Visibility**: Regularly attending industry events, conferences, and networking functions helps you get noticed by others in your field, including potential employers, colleagues, and leaders.

- **Personal Brand Building**: Networking allows you to establish a reputation within your industry as a knowledgeable, reliable, and resourceful professional, which can enhance your career prospects.

Networking should be seen as a long-term strategy for career growth. Building strong, genuine relationships with others can lead to unexpected opportunities.

# Ask MrCareer
## *101 Common Questions About Careers and Their Answers*

# #27 - How do I handle rejection when trying to move up?

Rejection is a natural part of career advancement. Here's how to handle it positively:

- Don't Take It Personally: Understand that rejection is often not a reflection of your abilities but rather a result of external factors like timing or the company's needs.

- Seek Feedback: After being rejected for a promotion or position, ask for constructive feedback. This can help you identify areas for improvement and increase your chances of success in the future.

- Stay Resilient: Maintain a positive attitude and stay focused on your long-term career goals. Use rejection as motivation to improve and keep striving for the next opportunity.

- Assess Your Approach: If you face repeated rejection, take a step back and evaluate your strategy. Consider whether you need additional skills, more visibility within the company, or a different approach in interviews or career conversations.

- Move Forward: Don't dwell on the rejection. Keep your energy focused on new opportunities and continue pursuing your career goals.

Handling rejection with grace and a willingness to learn can help you grow stronger and more prepared for future opportunities.

# Ask MrCareer
## *101 Common Questions About Careers and Their Answers*

# #28 - What is "imposter syndrome," and how can I overcome it?

Imposter syndrome is a psychological pattern where individuals doubt their accomplishments and feel like a fraud, despite evidence of their success. It's common in high-achieving individuals and can hold you back from advancing in your career. To overcome imposter syndrome:

- **Acknowledge Your Feelings**: Recognize that imposter syndrome is a common experience. By acknowledging it, you can begin to address it.

- **Focus on Your Achievements**: Keep track of your accomplishments, both big and small, to remind yourself of your capabilities. Celebrate your wins and give yourself credit for your successes.

- **Seek Support**: Talk to mentors or colleagues who can offer reassurance and perspective. Realizing that others have similar feelings can help normalize your experience.

- **Stop Comparing Yourself to Others**: Everyone has their own journey. Instead of comparing yourself to others, focus on your own progress and growth.

- **Learn from Mistakes**: Use challenges and setbacks as opportunities for growth, not as evidence of failure.

Overcoming imposter syndrome requires self-compassion, reflection on your strengths, and building confidence through positive reinforcement.

# Ask MrCareer
## *101 Common Questions About Careers and Their Answers*

# #29 - Should I consider a lateral move for career growth?

A lateral move refers to switching jobs within the same level or position in an organization, rather than moving up the corporate ladder (a promotion) or transitioning to a different field. While it might not involve an immediate increase in salary or authority, it can still play a significant role in career growth and development. Here are considerations for whether you should make a lateral move for career growth:

**1. Expanding Your Skillset**

- **Diversifying Experience**: A lateral move can allow you to gain exposure to new areas within your organization. For instance, if you're in a marketing role and are offered a lateral move to a product management position, it can broaden your understanding of how the business operates, giving you a well-rounded skillset that is attractive for future leadership roles.

- **Learning New Skills**: Lateral moves often involve stepping into different types of projects or responsibilities. If you're looking to develop specific skills that will help you in your long-term career, a lateral move can be a good opportunity to gain those skills without changing your entire career trajectory.

- **Building Versatility**: Having a broader range of competencies can make you more marketable in the future. In today's job market, employers value employees who can wear multiple hats and adapt to changing environments. Lateral moves can help you build this flexibility.

# Ask MrCareer
## *101 Common Questions About Careers and Their Answers*

### 2. Exploring New Interests

- **Pursuing Passion Projects**: If you've grown interested in a different aspect of your current field or organization, a lateral move might allow you to explore new areas of work that you're passionate about. This can lead to increased job satisfaction and personal fulfillment, which are important for long-term career happiness.

- **Avoiding Stagnation**: Staying in the same role for too long can result in burnout or boredom. A lateral move can reinvigorate your career by introducing new challenges, helping to keep you engaged and motivated in your work.

### 3. Building Your Network and Relationships

- **Expanding Your Professional Network**: Moving to a different department or role often means working with a new set of colleagues, managers, and stakeholders. These relationships can be valuable, expanding your internal network and increasing your visibility within the company.

- **Cross-Department Collaboration**: Lateral moves can offer opportunities to collaborate with different teams or departments. These cross-functional collaborations can give you insights into how the organization functions as a whole and build relationships that can be helpful if you decide to seek future promotions or leadership positions.

### 4. Improving Job Satisfaction

- **Avoiding Burnout or Discontent**: If you're feeling stuck or dissatisfied in your current position, a lateral move can refresh your career and help you avoid burnout. A new role can give you a different perspective, making your work feel more exciting and challenging.

# Ask MrCareer
## *101 Common Questions About Careers and Their Answers*

- **Finding Better Work-Life Balance**: In some cases, a lateral move can improve your work-life balance if the new role offers more flexible hours or a less stressful environment, even if the salary or title remains the same.

### 5. Weighing the Risks and Rewards

- **Lack of Immediate Financial Gain**: While a lateral move may not come with a pay raise or promotion, it could still be valuable in the long run. Consider the opportunity to learn, gain exposure, and build skills that can lead to greater career opportunities later.

- **Potential for Career Advancement**: A lateral move might position you better for future promotions or higher-paying roles. It's important to assess whether the new position has the potential to open up new avenues for upward mobility.

- **Organizational Culture and Fit**: If you're considering a move within your current organization, ensure that the new team or department aligns with your values and work style. A lateral move within an organization might bring you into a different organizational culture, which could be either a good or bad fit for you.

### Conclusion:

A lateral move can be a valuable strategy for career growth, especially if it helps you develop new skills, expand your professional network, or increase job satisfaction. While it may not offer immediate financial or positional benefits, the long-term career advantages can be significant. It's crucial to weigh your career goals and determine if the move aligns with your broader aspirations.

# Ask MrCareer
*101 Common Questions About Careers and Their Answers*

## #30 - How do I build a personal brand for my career?

Building a personal brand is essential for standing out in your field and establishing your professional identity. A well-crafted personal brand helps you communicate your values, expertise, and unique qualities to employers, colleagues, and potential clients, positioning you as an expert in your area. Here are steps to help you build a strong personal brand for your career:

### 1. Define Your Unique Value Proposition (UVP)

- **Identify Your Strengths**: Understand what makes you unique in your field. What skills or qualities do you possess that set you apart from others? This could be your technical expertise, leadership abilities, creativity, or problem-solving skills. The clearer you are about your strengths, the easier it will be to position yourself in your industry.

- **Clarify Your Purpose**: Reflect on what you want to achieve in your career and how you want others to perceive you. Do you want to be known for innovation, reliability, or your ability to deliver results? Identifying a clear purpose helps shape how you communicate your value to others.

### 2. Develop Your Online Presence

- **Create a Professional Online Profile**: One of the first steps in building a personal brand is creating an online presence that reflects your professional identity. Platforms like LinkedIn are essential for showcasing your qualifications, experience, and accomplishments. Make sure your profile is complete, including a professional photo, detailed work history, and relevant skills.

# Ask MrCareer
## *101 Common Questions About Careers and Their Answers*

- **Start a Personal Website or Blog**: If applicable, create a website or blog where you can showcase your work, projects, and achievements. A website serves as an online portfolio that is accessible to potential employers, clients, or collaborators. It also provides a platform for sharing your thoughts, insights, and expertise on industry trends or topics relevant to your career.

- **Engage on Social Media**: Use social media platforms like Twitter, Instagram, or professional groups to share industry-related content, comment on discussions, and engage with others in your field. Consistently sharing relevant and valuable content helps position you as a thought leader.

### 3. Share Your Expertise and Knowledge

- **Contribute to Industry Discussions**: Share your expertise by writing articles, giving talks, or participating in webinars or podcasts. This not only establishes you as an authority in your field but also helps you build credibility and visibility.

- **Offer Solutions to Problems**: Focus on providing value to others by solving problems in your industry. Whether it's offering advice to colleagues, creating tutorials, or sharing case studies, offering solutions reinforces your reputation as someone knowledgeable and reliable.

- **Publish Content**: Consider writing for industry blogs, contributing guest posts, or publishing content on platforms like Medium. This can help you gain recognition and build a following.

### 4. Network and Build Relationships

- **Attend Industry Events**: Networking is key to building a personal brand. Attend industry conferences, events, and seminars to meet new people and strengthen

# Ask MrCareer
## *101 Common Questions About Careers and Their Answers*

relationships. Face-to-face interactions often leave a lasting impression and can lead to future opportunities.

- **Join Professional Associations**: Becoming a member of relevant professional organizations or groups can increase your visibility and help you connect with like-minded professionals. These groups provide opportunities to collaborate and share your insights on a broader scale.

### 5. Develop Consistency and Authenticity

- **Consistency Across Platforms**: Ensure your personal brand is consistent across all platforms, whether it's your LinkedIn profile, personal website, or social media accounts. This consistency helps create a clear and unified message about who you are and what you stand for.

- **Be Authentic**: Authenticity is key to building trust and credibility. Don't try to be someone you're not in an attempt to please others or gain followers. Stay true to your values, beliefs, and expertise, as authenticity resonates with people and helps establish stronger connections.

### 6. Seek Feedback and Adjust

- **Request Feedback from Mentors or Peers**: Ask for feedback on how others perceive your personal brand. Their input can provide valuable insights on areas for improvement or things that you may not have considered.

- **Stay Open to Evolving**: Your personal brand should evolve as your career progresses. As you develop new skills or transition to new roles, update your brand to reflect these changes. Stay agile and adaptable to

# Ask MrCareer
## *101 Common Questions About Careers and Their Answers*

ensure your personal brand continues to align with your current goals and aspirations.

### 7. Be Visible and Accessible

- **Increase Visibility**: Take every opportunity to increase your visibility within your industry or organization. Volunteer for speaking opportunities, participate in online forums, or contribute to team projects. The more visible you are, the more likely you are to attract opportunities.

- **Be Accessible**: Building a personal brand also means being approachable. Whether it's offering help to others in your network or engaging in open conversations, make sure people feel they can connect with you and reach out for advice or collaboration.

### Conclusion:

Building a personal brand takes time and consistency, but it's a powerful tool for career advancement. By defining your unique value, establishing a strong online presence, networking, and continuously sharing your expertise, you can position yourself as an industry leader and open doors to new opportunities. A well-developed personal brand reflects your professional identity and makes you stand out in a competitive job market.

# Ask MrCareer
*101 Common Questions About Careers and Their Answers*

## Career Changes

#31- When is it time to change careers?

Changing careers is a big decision, and it's important to assess your personal and professional situation carefully. Here are signs it might be time to consider a career change:

- **Lack of Passion or Interest**: If you feel uninspired or uninterested in your work, or if it feels like a chore rather than a fulfilling pursuit, it may be time to explore a different career.

- **Burnout**: Chronic stress, exhaustion, or emotional fatigue from your current role may indicate it's no longer a good fit, and a career change could help restore your enthusiasm and energy.

- **Stagnation**: If you've reached a dead-end where there's little room for growth, challenge, or advancement in your current career, switching careers could give you new opportunities for growth.

- **Misalignment with Values**: If your current job doesn't align with your values or lifestyle goals, it may cause dissatisfaction. A career change allows you to find work that is more in line with your personal beliefs and aspirations.

- **Changing Interests**: Over time, your interests and goals may shift, and a career that once suited you may no longer be the best option. If you're interested in pursuing a passion or exploring a field that excites you, a career change can be the right move.

# Ask MrCareer
## *101 Common Questions About Careers and Their Answers*

- **Life Circumstances**: Major life changes like relocating, family changes, or personal growth can also make it the right time to change careers.

# Ask MrCareer
## *101 Common Questions About Careers and Their Answers*

## #32 - How do I transition into a completely new industry?

Transitioning into a completely new industry can be challenging but rewarding. Here's how you can approach it:

- Leverage Transferable Skills: Identify the skills from your current industry that can be applied to the new field, such as leadership, communication, problem-solving, or project management.

- Reskill or Upskill: Take courses, certifications, or attend workshops to gain the specific knowledge and skills required for the new industry. Online platforms like Coursera, LinkedIn Learning, and Udemy offer accessible options.

- Network with Industry Professionals: Build connections in the new industry by attending industry events, joining relevant groups on LinkedIn, or reaching out for informational interviews with people working in the field.

- Start with an Entry-Level Role: Be open to taking an entry-level position to learn the ropes and build experience in the new industry. This may mean accepting a pay cut initially, but it can provide valuable learning opportunities.

- Tailor Your Resume and Cover Letter: Customize your resume to highlight your transferable skills, relevant experience, and passion for the new field. Focus on how you can contribute to the industry and its challenges.

- Be Patient: Understand that transitioning to a new industry takes time, and setbacks may occur. Stay persistent and embrace the learning process.

# Ask MrCareer
*101 Common Questions About Careers and Their Answers*

## #33 - What challenges come with starting over in a career?

Starting over in a career can come with its fair share of challenges:

- **Loss of Seniority or Status**: If you're transitioning to a new industry or role, you may have to start at a lower level, which can feel like a loss of status or experience.

- **Skill Gaps**: You may not have the specific technical skills or knowledge required for the new field, which can make the transition challenging.

- **Building Credibility**: If you're entering a new industry, establishing credibility and earning the trust of colleagues and superiors can take time.

- **Financial Impact**: Starting over may mean accepting a lower salary or taking an initial pay cut, which can have short-term financial consequences.

- **Confidence Struggles**: Entering an unfamiliar field may shake your confidence, as you might feel out of place or uncertain about your ability to succeed.

- **Starting from Scratch**: Building a new professional network and reputation in a different industry can take time and effort, especially if you are shifting into a highly specialized field.

While challenging, starting over in a career can lead to significant personal and professional growth if approached with a clear plan and patience.

# Ask MrCareer
## *101 Common Questions About Careers and Their Answers*

# #34 - How can I leverage transferable skills for a career change?

When changing careers, transferable skills can be your greatest asset. These are skills you've developed in your current role that can be applied in a new career. Here's how to leverage them:

- **Identify Relevant Skills**: Look at your current skill set and determine which ones are applicable to your new career. For example, project management, leadership, communication, critical thinking, and problem-solving are often transferable across industries.

- **Highlight Your Experience**: In your resume and cover letter, emphasize these transferable skills by providing examples of how you've successfully applied them in your current job. Show how they can be valuable in the new role.

- **Tailor Your Pitch**: When networking or interviewing, tailor your pitch to focus on how your transferable skills make you a strong candidate for the new industry. Highlight the skills and experiences that will help you succeed in your new career.

- **Bridge the Gap with Education**: If there are gaps in your knowledge for the new role, use education (online courses, certifications, etc.) to complement your transferable skills and show your commitment to the new field.

- **Seek a Bridge Job**: Consider finding a job that serves as a transition between your old career and the new one, allowing you to apply your current skills while gaining experience in the new industry.

# Ask MrCareer
## *101 Common Questions About Careers and Their Answers*

By focusing on your transferable skills, you can show that you have the ability to succeed in a new career despite the lack of direct experience.

# Ask MrCareer
## *101 Common Questions About Careers and Their Answers*

# #35 - How do I overcome fear when switching careers?

Fear of switching careers is common, but there are ways to manage it:

- Research and Plan: Fear often comes from the unknown. By researching the new industry, understanding the required skills, and having a clear plan in place, you can minimize uncertainty and feel more confident.

- Start Small: Don't feel the need to make a dramatic change all at once. You can transition gradually by taking on freelance work, part-time jobs, or internships to build experience before fully committing.

- Seek Support: Talk to others who have made a similar career change or find a mentor who can guide you. Their experiences can help reassure you and provide insights into how to overcome common fears.

- Focus on the Benefits: Remind yourself of the reasons you want to make the change, whether it's a more fulfilling role, better work-life balance, or pursuing a passion. Keeping your motivations front and center can help combat fear.

- Embrace the Learning Curve: Understand that switching careers involves learning new things and making mistakes. This is normal and part of the growth process.

- Financial Safety Nets: If financial insecurity is a source of fear, create a buffer before making the switch. Save money, reduce unnecessary expenses, and explore side gigs to ease the financial strain during the transition.

# Ask MrCareer
## *101 Common Questions About Careers and Their Answers*

By taking these steps, you can reduce fear and feel more confident in making a successful career switch.

# Ask MrCareer
## *101 Common Questions About Careers and Their Answers*

## #36 - Is it better to be a specialist or a generalist?

The decision to be a specialist or a generalist depends on your career goals and the industry you're in. Both paths have their advantages:

- **Specialist**: Specializing allows you to become an expert in a specific area, which can make you highly sought after in niche industries. Specialists often command higher pay because of their expertise. However, the downside is that specialization can limit your job opportunities to a specific field.
    - **Advantages**: Higher pay, recognition as an expert, job security in niche industries.
    - **Disadvantages**: Fewer career options, potential for burnout if the industry changes or declines.
- **Generalist**: Being a generalist means having a broad skill set that allows you to work in various roles and industries. Generalists are adaptable and can easily pivot to different careers, making them valuable in industries that require flexibility.
    - **Advantages**: Greater job opportunities, adaptability, ability to transition between roles or industries.
    - **Disadvantages**: Lower earning potential compared to specialists, might lack in-depth expertise in any one area.

In summary, if you enjoy deep expertise and want to become a leader in a specific field, specialization may be for you. If you prefer variety and flexibility, being a generalist may be the better choice.

# Ask MrCareer
## *101 Common Questions About Careers and Their Answers*

## #37 - How do I handle a career gap?

A career gap doesn't have to be a roadblock. Here's how to handle it:

- **Be Honest and Transparent**: When explaining the gap in your resume, be honest but also focus on what you learned or accomplished during the time off (e.g., personal development, taking care of family, traveling, volunteering, or learning new skills).

- **Highlight Relevant Experiences**: Even if you weren't formally employed, highlight any freelance work, volunteer roles, courses, or personal projects you completed during the gap.

- **Network**: Networking can help you re-enter the job market more smoothly. Reach out to old colleagues, attend events, or join online communities in your field.

- **Up-skill During the Gap**: Take courses or certifications to stay relevant in your field and show potential employers that you've continued to develop your skills during the gap.

- **Confidence in Interviews**: In interviews, focus on what you bring to the table now, the skills you've gained, and why you're excited to return to work. Emphasize your readiness and commitment to your next role.

By framing the career gap as a positive experience, you can show potential employers that you've gained valuable skills and are eager to move forward in your career.

# Ask MrCareer
## *101 Common Questions About Careers and Their Answers*

## #38 - How do I explain a career change in an interview?

Explaining a career change in an interview requires framing it in a way that emphasizes your transferable skills and enthusiasm for the new direction:

- **Be Positive**: Focus on the positive aspects of your decision to change careers. Explain how the change aligns with your interests, values, and long-term career goals.

- **Emphasize Transferable Skills**: Highlight the skills from your previous career that will help you succeed in the new role. Show how your experience adds value and can be leveraged to make a meaningful impact.

- **Show Passion**: Demonstrate your excitement and passion for the new career. Employers want to see that you are genuinely interested and committed to your new path.

- **Address the Reason**: Be prepared to explain why you're making the switch, whether it's a desire for a more fulfilling role, better work-life balance, or the pursuit of a new challenge. Avoid negativity about your past career and focus on how the new job fits your aspirations.

# Ask MrCareer
## *101 Common Questions About Careers and Their Answers*

# #39 - Should I change careers if I feel unfulfilled?

If you feel unfulfilled in your current career, a change might be necessary, but it's important to consider a few things first:

- Evaluate the Source of Unfulfillment: Understand the root cause of your dissatisfaction. It could be a mismatch between your job and your values, work environment, lack of growth opportunities, or burnout. Identifying the exact issue can help you decide if a career change is necessary or if you just need to make adjustments in your current role.

- Consider Your Goals: Think about what would bring you fulfillment. Do you want to make a bigger impact, pursue a passion, or achieve a better work-life balance? A career change might be the answer if these goals are not attainable in your current career.

- Do Research: Explore other fields and industries to see if they align better with your interests and values. Sometimes, a lateral move or a minor adjustment can provide the fulfillment you're looking for without making a drastic career change.

Changing careers can bring fulfillment, but it's essential to be sure that it's the right move for you and that you're prepared to take on the challenges that come with it.

# Ask MrCareer
*101 Common Questions About Careers and Their Answers*

# #40 - How do I prepare financially for a career shift?

Preparing financially for a career shift is crucial to reduce stress and make a smoother transition:

- **Save Up an Emergency Fund**: Aim to have at least 3 to 6 months' worth of living expenses saved up. This will give you financial flexibility while you transition to a new job or career.

- **Evaluate Your Budget**: Take a close look at your finances to see where you can cut back or adjust your spending. This will allow you to live more comfortably during the transition period.

- **Consider Side Gigs**: If you can, consider starting a side business or freelance work in the new field before fully committing to the career change. This can help you build experience and generate income.

- **Look for Educational Assistance**: If additional education or training is needed, investigate scholarships, grants, or employer-sponsored programs that may help cover some of the costs.

- **Plan for Salary Changes**: Be aware that switching careers may initially involve a pay cut, so make sure your financial situation is flexible enough to accommodate this change.

# Ask MrCareer
## *101 Common Questions About Careers and Their Answers*

# Working from Home and Remote Careers

## #41 - What are the advantages and challenges of working from home?

**Advantages of Working from Home:**

1. **Flexibility**: One of the biggest advantages of working remotely is the flexibility it offers. You can often set your own schedule, which allows you to better balance personal and professional responsibilities. This can be especially beneficial for parents, caregivers, or anyone with a busy lifestyle.

2. **Cost Savings**: Working from home eliminates commuting costs, such as gas, public transportation fares, and parking. You may also save on work-related expenses like lunches, office attire, and professional dry cleaning.

3. **Increased Productivity**: Many remote workers report that they are more productive when working from home. With fewer distractions from coworkers and office noise, it's often easier to focus and complete tasks in a quieter, more personalized environment.

4. **Better Work-Life Balance**: With no commute and the ability to customize your workspace, remote work can lead to an improved work-life balance. This allows for more time to spend with family, pursue hobbies, or engage in self-care activities.

5. **Environmental Impact**: Working remotely can contribute to a reduction in your carbon footprint. Without

# Ask MrCareer
## *101 Common Questions About Careers and Their Answers*

commuting, there's less fuel consumption and fewer carbon emissions, helping the environment.

**Challenges of Working from Home:**

1. **Isolation**: One of the most common challenges of remote work is feeling isolated or disconnected from coworkers. The lack of face-to-face interaction can make it harder to build relationships, leading to loneliness or a sense of detachment.

2. **Distractions at Home**: While some find fewer distractions in a home office, others face distractions like household chores, children, pets, or roommates. Managing these distractions requires discipline and effective time management.

3. **Difficulty in Setting Boundaries**: Working from home can blur the lines between personal and professional life. Without a clear physical separation between work and home spaces, it can be challenging to "switch off" after working hours, leading to burnout or overwork.

4. **Technical Issues**: Remote work heavily relies on technology. Internet connectivity issues, software malfunctions, or lack of proper tools can disrupt productivity and cause frustration.

5. **Limited Career Advancement**: Some remote workers may feel that their career growth or professional development is slower than in-office colleagues. The lack of visibility in the workplace or less frequent interactions with leadership can make it more difficult to access opportunities for promotions or raises.

# Ask MrCareer
## *101 Common Questions About Careers and Their Answers*

# #42 - How do I stay productive in a remote career?

Staying productive in a remote career requires a combination of discipline, organization, and effective time management. Here are several strategies to boost productivity while working remotely:

1. **Create a Dedicated Workspace**: Designating a specific area for work can help you mentally separate work from personal life. This reduces distractions and helps you stay focused during work hours.

2. **Stick to a Routine**: Establish a daily schedule that includes time for breaks and meals. Setting a consistent start and end time to your workday helps reinforce work-life balance.

3. **Set Clear Goals**: Break your work down into daily, weekly, or monthly goals. Using task management tools like Trello, Asana, or Todoist can help you track progress and stay on target.

4. **Prioritize Tasks**: Focus on high-priority tasks first. Use techniques like the Pomodoro Method (working for 25-minute intervals with short breaks) to maintain focus throughout the day.

5. **Minimize Distractions**: Turn off notifications from social media, personal apps, or emails during work hours. Consider using website-blocking apps like Freedom or Cold Turkey to avoid browsing distractions.

6. **Leverage Technology**: Use tools for communication and collaboration (e.g., Zoom, Slack, Microsoft Teams) to stay connected with your team. Tools like Google Docs

or shared drive platforms help you collaborate efficiently without the need for in-person meetings.

7. **Take Regular Breaks**: Prevent burnout by scheduling short breaks throughout the day to stretch, walk around, or get fresh air. This helps maintain mental and physical energy for the long haul.

8. **Set Boundaries**: Establish clear work hours and stick to them. Inform family members or housemates of your availability to reduce interruptions during work time.

# Ask MrCareer
## 101 Common Questions About Careers and Their Answers

# #43 - How do I find legitimate work-from-home jobs?

Finding legitimate work-from-home jobs requires careful research and a critical approach to ensure the opportunities are legitimate and trustworthy. Here's how to go about it:

1. **Research Reputable Job Boards**: Some job boards specialize in remote work opportunities, such as We Work Remotely, Remote.co, FlexJobs, and Remote OK. These sites vet employers, reducing the likelihood of scams.

2. **Use Trusted Job Platforms**: Large, well-known job platforms like LinkedIn, Indeed, and Glassdoor also list remote positions. You can filter your search to show only remote or work-from-home jobs.

3. **Check Company Websites**: If there's a specific company you're interested in, check its careers page for remote opportunities. Many established companies are transitioning to remote or hybrid models.

4. **Avoid "Too Good to Be True" Offers**: Be cautious of job listings that promise high salaries for minimal work, especially if they ask for upfront fees for training or materials. Legitimate companies will never require you to pay to work for them.

5. **Read Reviews**: Look up reviews of companies on platforms like Glassdoor or Trustpilot to ensure they are legitimate and have a history of fair employment practices.

6. **Network**: Joining remote work communities or forums on platforms like Reddit or Facebook can provide

# Ask MrCareer
## *101 Common Questions About Careers and Their Answers*

recommendations and referrals from others already working remotely.

7. **Leverage Freelance Websites**: If you're open to contract or freelance work, websites like Upwork, Fiverr, or Freelancer.com can provide a variety of remote job options. These platforms allow you to build your portfolio and gain experience.

# Ask MrCareer
## *101 Common Questions About Careers and Their Answers*

# #44 - What skills are essential for remote work success?

Several skills are crucial for succeeding in a remote career. These skills help you navigate the challenges of working independently, managing time, and collaborating virtually:

1. **Time Management**: The ability to prioritize tasks, meet deadlines, and stay organized is essential when working remotely. Without direct supervision, you need to be able to manage your own schedule effectively.

2. **Self-Motivation and Discipline**: Remote workers need to stay motivated without the immediate oversight of an office environment. The ability to set goals, maintain focus, and push through distractions is key.

3. **Communication Skills**: Clear and concise communication is critical in a remote setting. You need to be able to express yourself effectively in emails, virtual meetings, and collaborative tools.

4. **Adaptability**: Remote work often requires adapting to new technologies, working with teams from different time zones, and being flexible with your schedule.

5. **Technical Proficiency**: Comfort with technology is essential, especially when working with cloud-based tools, communication platforms (e.g., Zoom, Slack), project management software (e.g., Trello, Asana), and productivity tools.

6. **Problem-Solving Skills**: In the absence of direct supervision, remote workers must be able to tackle challenges independently. Creative problem-solving and critical thinking are essential for overcoming obstacles without relying on others for immediate support.

# Ask MrCareer
## *101 Common Questions About Careers and Their Answers*

7. **Collaboration and Teamwork**: While remote work can be isolating, it still requires the ability to work as part of a virtual team. Collaboration skills, including the ability to coordinate and communicate across different time zones, are vital.

8. **Tech Troubleshooting**: Basic knowledge of how to troubleshoot common technical problems (e.g., connectivity issues, software malfunctions) will save time and reduce dependence on IT support.

# Ask MrCareer
## *101 Common Questions About Careers and Their Answers*

# #45 - How can I maintain work-life balance while working remotely

Maintaining a healthy work-life balance when working from home can be challenging but is essential for preventing burnout and maintaining well-being. Here are strategies to help achieve that balance:

1. **Set Clear Work Hours**: Define specific hours for starting and finishing work each day. Stick to this routine as much as possible to avoid overworking or letting work bleed into your personal time.

2. **Create Physical Boundaries**: If possible, set up a dedicated workspace that is separate from areas where you relax or engage in hobbies. This helps your brain associate certain spaces with work and others with relaxation.

3. **Take Regular Breaks**: Use the Pomodoro technique or simply step away from your desk every hour to stretch, take a walk, or do something non-work-related. These breaks help reduce stress and recharge your focus.

4. **Prioritize Tasks**: At the start of each day, prioritize your tasks and focus on completing the most important ones first. This helps ensure that you stay productive during work hours and can enjoy your personal time without worry.

5. **Set Boundaries with Family and Friends**: Communicate your work schedule to others in your household to reduce interruptions during work hours. Having a designated space and routine makes it easier to stay focused when needed.

# Ask MrCareer
## *101 Common Questions About Careers and Their Answers*

6. **Establish Personal Time**: Schedule personal activities such as exercise, hobbies, or social time, and make sure to protect these hours. Treat them as equally important as work tasks to maintain balance.

7. **Avoid Multitasking**: Focus on one task at a time during your work hours, and don't try to juggle household chores or errands while working. Multitasking can lead to lower productivity and increase stress.

8. **Unplug After Work**: When your workday is over, physically step away from your workspace. Turn off work-related

# Ask MrCareer
*101 Common Questions About Careers and Their Answers*

## Entrepreneurship and Freelancing

### #46 - Should I start my own business or stick to employment?

Choosing between starting your own business and staying in employment depends on several personal and professional factors. Each option has distinct advantages and challenges.

**Advantages of Employment:**

1. **Stability and Security**: Employment offers predictable income, benefits (such as health insurance, retirement plans), and job security, especially in well-established companies.

2. **Work-Life Balance**: Typically, employees work within set hours and have more predictable days off, allowing for a clearer separation between work and personal life.

3. **Less Risk**: There's less financial risk in a salaried job, as employees don't have to invest their own capital or deal with the responsibilities of running a business.

4. **Professional Development**: Employers often provide training, mentorship, and opportunities for growth, making it easier for employees to expand their skill set.

**Advantages of Entrepreneurship:**

1. **Independence**: Business owners have the freedom to set their own schedules, make decisions, and shape their company's direction.

2. **Potential for Growth**: Entrepreneurship allows for the possibility of greater financial rewards and the

# Ask MrCareer
## *101 Common Questions About Careers and Their Answers*

opportunity to scale a business beyond what a job might offer.

3. **Creative Control**: Entrepreneurs can bring their vision to life and follow their passions without having to adhere to someone else's structure or goals.

4. **Flexibility**: Running your own business often offers flexibility in how and when work is completed, which can be appealing for those with specific personal needs or goals.

Ultimately, the decision hinges on one's risk tolerance, financial situation, goals, and desire for independence. Some may thrive in a structured environment, while others may find entrepreneurship more fulfilling despite its inherent challenges.

# Ask MrCareer
## *101 Common Questions About Careers and Their Answers*

# #47 - What are the first steps to becoming an entrepreneur?

Becoming an entrepreneur involves several important steps to ensure that the business venture has a solid foundation. Here's how to start:

1. **Identify a Business Idea**: The first step is to identify a product or service that addresses a market need or solves a problem. Research the industry to ensure there's demand and potential for growth.

2. **Conduct Market Research**: Analyze your target market, competitors, and customer needs. This helps refine the business idea and ensures it's viable.

3. **Create a Business Plan**: Develop a detailed business plan outlining your goals, target market, marketing strategies, financial projections, and operational plans. This serves as a roadmap for the business and helps secure funding.

4. **Secure Financing**: Determine how you will fund your business. This may involve using personal savings, securing loans, or seeking investors.

5. **Register the Business**: Choose a business name and legal structure (sole proprietorship, LLC, corporation) and file the necessary paperwork with local or national authorities.

6. **Set Up Operations**: Purchase the equipment, hire staff (if needed), and establish systems for product or service delivery.

7. **Market Your Business**: Start marketing through both online and offline channels. Create a website, utilize

# Ask MrCareer
## *101 Common Questions About Careers and Their Answers*

social media, and consider traditional marketing methods to reach potential customers.

8. **Prepare for Challenges**: Be prepared to face difficulties, such as financial pressures, time constraints, and competition. Cultivate resilience and a willingness to adapt.

# Ask MrCareer
## *101 Common Questions About Careers and Their Answers*

# #48 - How do I transition from a full-time job to freelancing?

Transitioning from full-time employment to freelancing requires planning and preparation to ensure a smooth and sustainable career shift. Here are the key steps:

1. **Build a Strong Portfolio**: Before leaving your full-time job, build a portfolio showcasing your work. This can be in the form of a personal website, a social media presence, or other platforms that highlight your skills and accomplishments.

2. **Set Financial Expectations**: Freelancing can come with income fluctuations, so ensure you have sufficient savings to cover living expenses for a few months while you build a client base.

3. **Start Freelancing on the Side**: If possible, begin freelancing part-time while still employed. This allows you to test the waters, gain experience, and build relationships with clients.

4. **Create a Business Structure**: As a freelancer, you're essentially running a business. Set up an invoicing system, business bank accounts, and tax records. Consider forming a legal business entity for tax and liability purposes.

5. **Build Your Network**: Leverage your existing professional network to find freelance opportunities. Attend industry events, join online forums, or use freelance platforms to connect with potential clients.

6. **Set Clear Boundaries**: As a freelancer, you'll need to manage your time effectively. Set clear work hours,

# Ask MrCareer
## *101 Common Questions About Careers and Their Answers*

deadlines, and communicate your availability with clients to maintain a balance between work and personal life.

7. **Secure Your First Clients**: Use your portfolio and network to attract your first few clients. Offer services at competitive rates to establish credibility and build testimonials.

8. **Transition Gradually**: Don't leave your full-time job until you have enough freelance work to support yourself financially. A gradual transition allows you to adapt without taking on too much risk.

# Ask MrCareer
## *101 Common Questions About Careers and Their Answers*

## #49 - What challenges do freelancers face?

Freelancing offers flexibility, but it also comes with its own set of challenges:

1. **Income Instability**: Freelancers often face irregular income streams. The lack of a steady paycheck means that some months may be financially tight, especially when just starting out.

2. **Client Acquisition**: Building a reliable client base can take time. Freelancers often spend a significant amount of time marketing themselves, pitching to clients, and securing contracts.

3. **Lack of Benefits**: Unlike traditional employees, freelancers don't have employer-sponsored health insurance, retirement plans, or paid time off. This requires freelancers to manage their own benefits and plan for their financial future.

4. **Isolation**: Working alone without a team can lead to feelings of loneliness or lack of collaboration. Freelancers must find ways to stay motivated and connected, such as joining online communities or co-working spaces.

5. **Time Management**: Freelancers must juggle multiple clients, deadlines, and administrative tasks. Managing time effectively between delivering work and handling business responsibilities can be challenging.

6. **Legal and Tax Issues**: Freelancers are responsible for their own taxes, business licenses, and legal matters. They must keep track of income, expenses, and tax deductions while staying compliant with regulations.

# Ask MrCareer
## *101 Common Questions About Careers and Their Answers*

7. **Work-Life Balance**: When working from home, it can be difficult to separate work from personal life, leading to burnout or overwork. Establishing boundaries is essential for maintaining balance.

# Ask MrCareer
## *101 Common Questions About Careers and Their Answers*

## #50 - How do I market myself as a freelancer?

Marketing is essential for attracting clients and growing a freelance business. Here's how to do it effectively:

1. **Create a Strong Online Presence**: Build a website or portfolio showcasing your work, services, and testimonials. Include your contact information, clear descriptions of what you offer, and a professional photo.

2. **Leverage Social Media**: Use platforms like LinkedIn, Instagram, or Twitter to share your work, connect with potential clients, and demonstrate your expertise. Regularly post content relevant to your field.

3. **Network with Industry Professionals**: Attend industry events (either virtually or in-person), join online forums or groups, and collaborate with other professionals in your field to increase your visibility.

4. **Offer Referrals or Discounts**: Encourage clients to refer you by offering incentives. You can also offer introductory discounts for new clients or package deals to attract more business.

5. **Utilize Freelance Platforms**: Websites like Upwork, Fiverr, and Freelancer.com allow freelancers to find clients in a structured environment. Ensure your profile is detailed and well-written, highlighting your skills.

6. **Ask for Testimonials and Reviews**: After completing successful projects, ask clients for reviews or testimonials. Positive feedback helps establish credibility and trust with potential clients.

7. **Create Valuable Content**: Start a blog, offer free resources, or create videos to showcase your expertise.

# Ask MrCareer
## *101 Common Questions About Careers and Their Answers*

Providing value upfront can attract leads and position you as a thought leader.

8. **Email Marketing**: Build an email list and keep in touch with past and potential clients. Offer updates, promotions, and valuable content through a regular newsletter.

# Ask MrCareer
## *101 Common Questions About Careers and Their Answers*

# #51 - Is entrepreneurship a good career choice for everyone?

Entrepreneurship is not a one-size-fits-all career choice. While it can be rewarding and offer significant personal and financial freedom, it also presents many risks. Here's what to consider:

1. **Risk Tolerance**: Entrepreneurs must be willing to take financial and personal risks. Starting and running a business often involves uncertainty, and not everyone is comfortable with that level of risk.

2. **Self-Motivation and Discipline**: Entrepreneurs must have the self-drive to stay focused on their goals and consistently work toward building their business, even when there are setbacks.

3. **Financial Stability**: Entrepreneurs should have access to financial resources, whether through savings, loans, or investors, as launching a business can be expensive.

4. **Problem-Solving Skills**: Entrepreneurship requires constant problem-solving. Entrepreneurs face a variety of challenges, from operational issues to market shifts, and they need to navigate these with resourcefulness.

5. **Passion and Vision**: Successful entrepreneurs often have a clear passion or vision driving them. This motivation can sustain them through the inevitable ups and downs of business ownership.

6. **Support System**: Having a supportive network of family, friends, mentors, or business partners can make a significant difference in an entrepreneur's success.

Entrepreneurship is a good fit for those who are willing to take on challenges, have the necessary skills, and are passionate

# Ask MrCareer
## *101 Common Questions About Careers and Their Answers*

about building something of their own. For others, a more structured career in employment may be more suitable.

# Ask MrCareer
## *101 Common Questions About Careers and Their Answers*

# #52 - How do I manage income uncertainty as a freelancer?

Managing income uncertainty is one of the biggest challenges of freelancing. Here's how to handle it:

1. **Set Aside Emergency Savings**: Aim to have 3-6 months of living expenses saved up to cover periods when work is scarce.

2. **Diversify Your Client Base**: Work with a variety of clients to avoid relying too heavily on one source of income. This can help minimize the impact if a client drops off.

3. **Set Clear Payment Terms**: Establish clear payment schedules and terms with clients, including upfront deposits, payment upon delivery, or regular retainer agreements.

4. **Budget Wisely**: Keep track of your expenses and income, and live below your means when times are good so you can manage periods of income drought.

5. **Create Multiple Revenue Streams**: Offer different services, or create passive income streams such as courses, e-books, or digital products. This can stabilize your cash flow.

6. **Manage Taxes Carefully**: Freelancers must handle their own taxes, so it's important to set aside a portion of each payment to cover tax liabilities. Work with an accountant to estimate and plan for taxes.

# Ask MrCareer
## *101 Common Questions About Careers and Their Answers*

# #53 - How do I know if I'm ready to start my own business?

Determining if you're ready to start a business involves self-assessment and careful planning. Here are some signs that you may be prepared:

1. **You have a Clear Idea**: If you have a solid business idea or concept with a clear target market, you may be ready.

2. **You've Done Research**: You've researched your industry, competitors, and potential customers, and you understand the challenges and opportunities of the market.

3. **You're Financially Prepared**: You've saved enough money to cover startup costs and have a plan for funding the business in the early stages.

4. **You Have the Necessary Skills**: You possess the skills required to run a business or are willing to learn about marketing, sales, finances, and operations.

5. **You Have a Support System**: You have support from mentors, family, or partners to help guide you through the entrepreneurial process.

If you check most of these boxes, it's likely that you're ready to take the leap.

# Ask MrCareer
## *101 Common Questions About Careers and Their Answers*

# #54 - What industries are best for entrepreneurs?

Certain industries are particularly ripe for entrepreneurship due to market trends, growth potential, or consumer demand. Some of the best industries include:

1. **Technology and Software**: With increasing reliance on technology, there are opportunities in software development, IT consulting, cybersecurity, app development, and SaaS products.

2. **E-commerce**: The online shopping boom continues, and entrepreneurs can succeed in dropshipping, creating niche products, or running online stores.

3. **Health and Wellness**: As people focus more on health, fitness, mental wellness, and organic food, there are opportunities in personal training, health coaching, and wellness products.

4. **Sustainability**: As environmental concerns grow, businesses focused on sustainable practices, green energy, recycling, or eco-friendly products are gaining popularity.

5. **Education and E-learning**: Online courses, coaching, tutoring services, and educational tools are in demand as people seek flexible and accessible learning opportunities.

6. **Digital Marketing**: Businesses in search of online visibility create demand for SEO, social media marketing, content marketing, and other digital marketing services.

# Ask MrCareer
## *101 Common Questions About Careers and Their Answers*

7. **Real Estate**: Real estate continues to offer opportunities for property management, investment, or consulting services.

The best industry depends on your expertise, interests, and the market conditions of your region.

# Ask MrCareer
*101 Common Questions About Careers and Their Answers*

# #55 - How can I stay motivated as a self-employed professional?

Staying motivated as a self-employed professional can be difficult when you don't have a boss or set work hours. Here's how to stay driven:

1. **Set Clear Goals**: Establish short-term and long-term goals to give your work direction. Break larger goals into smaller, achievable tasks.

2. **Create a Routine**: Establish a daily schedule that includes work hours, breaks, and personal time. Having a structured day can help maintain focus.

3. **Celebrate Wins**: Recognize and reward yourself for achieving milestones, whether that's completing a project or landing a new client.

4. **Stay Organized**: Use productivity tools like calendars, to-do lists, and time trackers to stay on top of deadlines and tasks.

5. **Join a Community**: Network with other self-employed professionals, either online or locally, for motivation and support.

6. **Keep Learning**: Stay engaged by learning new skills, attending workshops, or expanding your expertise. This helps prevent burnout and keeps you interested in your work.

7. **Work-Life Balance**: Don't let work consume all of your time. Set boundaries and prioritize personal well-being, hobbies, and relationships.

# Ask MrCareer
## *101 Common Questions About Careers and Their Answers*

By staying organized, setting goals, and maintaining a balance between work and life, you can keep your motivation high as a self-employed professional.

# Ask MrCareer
## *101 Common Questions About Careers and Their Answers*

# Work-Life Balance and Career Satisfaction

## #56 - How do I balance my career and personal life?

Balancing career and personal life is a common challenge, but it can be achieved with thoughtful strategies. Here are some key tips:

1. **Set Boundaries**: Establish clear boundaries between work and personal time. Avoid checking emails or working outside of your designated work hours. Let family or friends know when you are working and when you are available for personal activities.

2. **Prioritize Tasks**: Identify and prioritize your most important tasks for both work and personal life. Use tools like to-do lists or planners to manage your time effectively.

3. **Learn to Say No**: Don't overcommit yourself to work or personal events. Recognize your limits and decline tasks or invitations that will overwhelm you.

4. **Delegate Responsibilities**: In both your professional and personal life, delegate tasks when possible. At work, assign responsibilities to team members. At home, share household duties with family members or hire help if needed.

5. **Take Breaks**: Incorporate breaks into your day to recharge, whether at work or at home. Taking short

# Ask MrCareer
## *101 Common Questions About Careers and Their Answers*

breaks helps to maintain focus and energy throughout the day.

6. **Make Time for Self-Care**: Regular exercise, hobbies, relaxation, and quality sleep are essential for maintaining a balanced life. Make time for activities that restore your energy and keep you healthy.

By effectively managing time and setting boundaries, you can enjoy a fulfilling career while maintaining a healthy personal life.

# Ask MrCareer
## *101 Common Questions About Careers and Their Answers*

## #57 - What does "career satisfaction" mean?

Career satisfaction refers to the fulfillment or contentment you feel about your work, including both the external rewards (such as salary, benefits, and recognition) and the intrinsic rewards (such as personal growth, a sense of purpose, and job engagement). Key aspects of career satisfaction include:

1. **Alignment with Values**: When your work aligns with your personal values, you feel more satisfied and motivated.

2. **Work-Life Balance**: A career that allows you to balance your professional responsibilities with personal commitments contributes to overall satisfaction.

3. **Growth and Development**: Opportunities for learning, skill development, and career advancement increase satisfaction by providing a sense of achievement and progress.

4. **Autonomy and Recognition**: Having control over your work and being recognized for your contributions fosters satisfaction.

5. **Positive Work Environment**: A supportive work culture, good relationships with colleagues, and a healthy work atmosphere contribute to job satisfaction.

Career satisfaction varies by individual preferences, but achieving a sense of purpose and balance often plays a major role.

# Ask MrCareer
## *101 Common Questions About Careers and Their Answers*

## #58 - How do I avoid career burnout?

Career burnout is a state of physical, emotional, and mental exhaustion caused by prolonged stress. To avoid burnout, consider these strategies:

1. **Manage Workload**: Set realistic goals and avoid taking on more work than you can handle. Use time management techniques to prioritize tasks effectively.

2. **Take Regular Breaks**: Short breaks throughout the day help you recharge and maintain productivity. Avoid working through lunch or staying late every day.

3. **Practice Self-Care**: Engage in physical activity, meditation, or hobbies to reduce stress. Maintaining your physical and mental well-being helps prevent burnout.

4. **Set Boundaries**: Learn to say no to additional tasks or responsibilities when your plate is full. Avoid taking work home or checking work emails outside office hours.

5. **Seek Support**: Talk to a manager, mentor, or counselor if you're feeling overwhelmed. Open communication helps to resolve stressors before they escalate.

6. **Take Time Off**: Use vacation days or personal days to disconnect from work and rest. Taking breaks away from work can help you regain perspective and energy.

By setting boundaries, managing workload, and taking care of yourself, you can protect yourself from burnout.

# Ask MrCareer
## *101 Common Questions About Careers and Their Answers*

# #59 - Should I prioritize work or family when conflicts arise?

When work and family conflicts arise, prioritizing one over the other depends on the situation, but here are general considerations:

1. **Assess Urgency**: If a family member is sick or facing a crisis, family obligations often take precedence. If there is an urgent work deadline, it may require short-term prioritization of work.

2. **Long-Term Perspective**: Consider the long-term impact of your decision. Constantly prioritizing work over family can strain relationships and well-being, while neglecting work may hurt career progression.

3. **Work Flexibility**: Many workplaces offer flexibility, such as remote work or flexible hours. If you can adjust your work schedule to accommodate family needs, this might be a solution.

4. **Open Communication**: Communicate with both your employer and family members to express your needs. Let your employer know when family issues arise, and discuss possible adjustments.

5. **Evaluate Priorities**: Regularly evaluate your personal and professional goals. If family or work demands are overwhelming, it might be time to reassess priorities and explore ways to achieve a better balance.

Ultimately, balance is key. Make decisions based on your values and the immediate needs of both work and family.

# Ask MrCareer
*101 Common Questions About Careers and Their Answers*

# #60 - How do I handle stress in high-pressure careers?

Stress management is essential in high-pressure careers. Here are strategies to cope effectively:

1. **Stay Organized**: Prioritize tasks and break them into smaller, manageable steps. This prevents feeling overwhelmed by large projects.

2. **Practice Mindfulness**: Mindfulness techniques, such as deep breathing, meditation, or taking breaks to refocus, can help reduce stress levels.

3. **Manage Time Effectively**: Use time management tools to ensure you're using your time wisely and aren't caught in a rush. Allocate specific time blocks for each task.

4. **Seek Support**: Talk to colleagues, mentors, or supervisors if you're feeling overwhelmed. Sometimes discussing the issue can provide clarity and reduce stress.

5. **Focus on What You Can Control**: In high-pressure situations, focus on the aspects of your work that you can control. Accept that some factors are outside your control.

6. **Exercise and Rest**: Physical activity is a great way to relieve stress. Exercise regularly to stay healthy and relieve built-up tension.

7. **Set Realistic Expectations**: Set achievable goals, and don't expect perfection. Understand your limits and work within them.

# Ask MrCareer
## *101 Common Questions About Careers and Their Answers*

# Career and Education

## #61 - Is a college degree necessary for a successful career?

A college degree is not always necessary for a successful career, but it can provide several benefits:

1. **Skill Development**: College offers structured learning and development of critical thinking, problem-solving, and specific skills that can be valuable in many careers.

2. **Career Opportunities**: Many industries still require a degree as a minimum qualification for certain positions. However, there are many fields where experience and skills can substitute for formal education.

3. **Networking**: College can provide networking opportunities with peers, professors, and industry professionals that can benefit your career.

4. **Alternative Education**: Certifications, boot camps, apprenticeships, and on-the-job training can provide the necessary skills for many careers without a degree.

Ultimately, success depends on skills, experience, and networking, which can be gained both with or without a college degree.

# Ask MrCareer
## *101 Common Questions About Careers and Their Answers*

# #62 - What are alternative career paths for those without degrees?

There are many career paths that don't require a degree but still offer opportunities for success:

1. **Skilled Trades**: Electricians, plumbers, HVAC technicians, and other skilled trades often require apprenticeships or certifications rather than a degree.

2. **Technology**: Careers in web development, coding, and IT support can be started through coding boot camps, certifications, or self-taught skills.

3. **Sales and Marketing**: Sales positions, including real estate agents and digital marketing specialists, often require experience and skills over formal education.

4. **Creative Fields**: Graphic design, photography, writing, and other creative fields value portfolios and experience more than degrees.

5. **Entrepreneurship**: Starting your own business can be a successful alternative career path, leveraging practical skills and industry knowledge instead of formal education.

6. **Health and Fitness**: Personal trainers, yoga instructors, and nutritionists can pursue certification programs rather than a degree.

Alternative career paths often require a willingness to learn and build skills through hands-on experience or specialized training.

# Ask MrCareer
## *101 Common Questions About Careers and Their Answers*

# #63 - How do I choose the right major for my career goals?

Choosing the right major involves a combination of self-reflection and research:

1. **Assess Your Interests**: Start by evaluating your personal interests and passions. What subjects or activities excite you? Aligning your major with something you enjoy will make it easier to stay motivated.

2. **Understand Your Strengths**: Consider your skills and strengths. Are you good at problem-solving, creative thinking, or working with people? Choose a major that matches your abilities.

3. **Research Career Opportunities**: Explore potential careers related to various majors. Research the job market and opportunities in fields you're considering. Consider earning potential, job growth, and career satisfaction in each field.

4. **Seek Guidance**: Talk to academic advisors, professionals in the industry, or mentors who can provide insights into different majors and their career prospects.

5. **Experiment**: Take introductory courses in different fields to get a feel for what interests you. This can help you make a more informed decision.

Choosing the right major is an important decision that should align with your long-term goals, skills, and interests.

# Ask MrCareer
*101 Common Questions About Careers and Their Answers*

# #64- How do I balance work and further education?

Balancing work and education requires careful time management and prioritization:

1. **Set Clear Priorities**: Determine your top priorities and understand that balancing work and education will require effort from both sides. Be prepared to adjust when necessary.

2. **Create a Schedule**: Plan out your work and study hours in advance. Allocate specific times for studying, attending classes, and working to stay organized.

3. **Use Flexible Learning Options**: If possible, opt for online classes, night classes, or weekend programs that offer flexibility around your work schedule.

4. **Stay Organized**: Use planners or digital tools to manage both your work responsibilities and educational commitments. Keep track of deadlines, exams, and assignments.

5. **Communicate with Employers**: Talk to your employer about your educational commitments. Some employers may offer flexible hours or even financial support for further education.

6. **Take Care of Yourself**: Don't neglect self-care. Make sure you get enough rest, eat well, and exercise to maintain your physical and mental health.

Balancing work and education requires discipline and time management, but it can be done successfully with proper planning.

# Ask MrCareer
*101 Common Questions About Careers and Their Answers*

# #65 - What role do internships play in launching a career?

Internships play a crucial role in gaining real-world experience and can significantly enhance your career prospects:

1. **Hands-On Experience**: Internships provide hands-on experience in a professional environment, helping you apply theoretical knowledge to practical situations.

2. **Networking Opportunities**: Internships allow you to connect with industry professionals and build a network of contacts that can help you in your job search after graduation.

3. **Skill Development**: Interns develop valuable skills such as communication, teamwork, and problem-solving, which are attractive to future employers.

4. **Resume Building**: Having internship experience on your resume demonstrates initiative and commitment, making you stand out in the competitive job market.

5. **Potential Job Offers**: Many companies hire their interns full-time after they graduate. Internships can lead to permanent positions if you perform well.

Internships are valuable tools for building experience, developing skills, and increasing employability.

# Ask MrCareer
## *101 Common Questions About Careers and Their Answers*

# Challenges in Careers

## #66 - How do I handle a toxic work environment?

A toxic work environment can severely affect your well-being and job satisfaction. Here's how to handle it:

1. **Identify the Problem**: Recognize the signs of toxicity, such as constant negativity, bullying, favoritism, or unrealistic expectations. Acknowledging the issue is the first step.

2. **Set Boundaries**: If possible, limit your interactions with toxic individuals or teams. Set clear emotional boundaries and try not to internalize negativity.

3. **Seek Support**: Talk to trusted colleagues, a supervisor, or a mentor about the toxic environment. They may offer advice or help address the situation.

4. **Document Incidents**: Keep a record of toxic behavior, especially if it involves harassment or discrimination. Documentation can be useful if you need to escalate the issue.

5. **Focus on Self-Care**: Make sure to take care of your mental and physical health. Engage in activities that help you manage stress, such as exercise, meditation, or hobbies.

6. **Consider Escalation**: If the situation doesn't improve, consider approaching HR or higher management. Present your concerns professionally and constructively.

# Ask MrCareer
## *101 Common Questions About Careers and Their Answers*

7. **Evaluate Your Options**: If the environment remains intolerable despite efforts, it may be time to consider looking for a new job or transferring within the company.

Protecting your well-being is paramount. Addressing toxicity head-on can help, but sometimes leaving the environment may be the healthiest option.

# Ask MrCareer
## *101 Common Questions About Careers and Their Answers*

# #67 - What should I do if I feel stuck in my career?

Feeling stuck in your career can be frustrating, but there are ways to break free:

1. **Self-Reflection**: Take time to assess what's making you feel stuck. Are you bored with your work, lacking challenges, or dissatisfied with your growth? Understanding the root cause will help you find a solution.

2. **Set New Goals**: Reevaluate your professional goals. Are they still aligned with your passions and aspirations? Set short- and long-term goals to guide your next steps.

3. **Seek Feedback**: Talk to your manager, mentor, or trusted colleagues about your performance and areas for improvement. Constructive feedback can provide a clearer path forward.

4. **Learn New Skills**: Take a course or certification in your field to develop new skills. This can increase your value and open up new opportunities.

5. **Network**: Expand your professional network to learn about other career opportunities or industries. Networking can help you discover potential job openings or new paths.

6. **Consider a Lateral Move**: If upward mobility seems limited, look for opportunities to switch roles within the organization. A lateral move can offer new challenges and growth.

7. **Explore New Career Paths**: If you feel truly uninspired, it may be time to consider a career shift. Conduct

# Ask MrCareer
## *101 Common Questions About Careers and Their Answers*

research, talk to industry professionals, and explore options that excite you.

When you feel stuck, taking proactive steps to reassess your situation and make changes can lead to new opportunities.

# Ask MrCareer
*101 Common Questions About Careers and Their Answers*

# #68 - How do I deal with workplace discrimination

Workplace discrimination is unacceptable and should be addressed:

1. **Document the Discrimination**: Keep detailed records of discriminatory actions, including dates, times, what occurred, and any witnesses. This documentation will be valuable if you decide to escalate the issue.

2. **Confront the Issue**: If you feel safe doing so, consider addressing the discriminatory behavior directly with the person involved. Use "I" statements to express how their actions make you feel.

3. **Talk to HR**: If the issue continues, report the discrimination to HR. Present your documentation clearly and professionally. HR is responsible for ensuring a discrimination-free workplace.

4. **Know Your Rights**: Familiarize yourself with your legal rights regarding discrimination. If you're in the U.S., laws such as the Civil Rights Act and Equal Employment Opportunity laws protect against workplace discrimination.

5. **Seek Legal Advice**: If the discrimination is severe or ongoing, consult an attorney specializing in employment law to understand your options and potential actions.

6. **Support System**: Seek emotional and professional support from colleagues, mentors, or external support groups. Handling discrimination alone can be overwhelming, so don't hesitate to reach out.

# Ask MrCareer
## *101 Common Questions About Careers and Their Answers*

Dealing with workplace discrimination requires courage and a systematic approach, but it's crucial to protect your rights and well-being.

# Ask MrCareer
## *101 Common Questions About Careers and Their Answers*

## #69 - How do I stay motivated in a stagnant job?

Staying motivated in a stagnant job can be challenging, but there are ways to maintain drive:

1. **Set Personal Goals**: Even if your job lacks growth opportunities, create personal professional goals such as improving a skill, learning something new, or completing projects efficiently.

2. **Seek Challenges**: Look for tasks or projects that allow you to stretch your abilities. Volunteer for new assignments or responsibilities to stay engaged.

3. **Find Meaning**: Focus on the parts of your job that align with your values or passions. Even mundane tasks can be fulfilling if you connect them to your personal purpose.

4. **Build Relationships**: Cultivate strong relationships with colleagues. Having a positive work environment and supportive connections can boost motivation and morale.

5. **Request Feedback**: Ask for feedback on your performance to understand areas where you can improve. Constructive criticism can reignite motivation.

6. **Take Care of Yourself**: Avoid burnout by balancing work with self-care. Healthy habits like regular exercise, taking breaks, and managing stress can maintain your energy and motivation.

If you focus on personal growth, find meaning in your tasks, and seek new challenges, you can stay motivated despite stagnation.

# Ask MrCareer
## *101 Common Questions About Careers and Their Answers*

# #70 - How do I deal with being overqualified for jobs?

Being overqualified for a job can be frustrating, but here's how to handle it:

1. **Reframe the Situation**: View your overqualification as a strength. Highlight how your experience can bring value to the company, such as improving efficiency or mentoring colleagues.

2. **Align Expectations**: When applying, emphasize your flexibility and willingness to take on the role. Make it clear that you're not seeking to replace someone or move up quickly but are genuinely interested in the job.

3. **Avoid Overwhelming Employers**: When discussing your qualifications, avoid presenting yourself as someone who will quickly get bored or need constant challenges. Focus on the aspects of the job that excite you.

4. **Address Concerns in Interviews**: Be prepared to discuss your overqualification in interviews. Explain why you are interested in the role, how you plan to stay engaged, and how your experience can benefit the team.

5. **Look for Ways to Grow**: Even in a role where you're overqualified, find ways to expand your skills, such as working on diverse projects, improving team dynamics, or taking on leadership roles.

If you're overqualified, positioning your experience as an asset and focusing on job satisfaction rather than titles can help overcome potential concerns.

# Ask MrCareer
*101 Common Questions About Careers and Their Answers*

# Future of Work

## #71 - What are the careers of the future?

The careers of the future are driven by technological advancements and changing societal needs. Some promising fields include:

1. **Artificial Intelligence and Machine Learning**: With AI continuing to evolve, careers in data science, machine learning engineering, and AI research are in high demand.

2. **Healthcare and Biotechnology**: The aging population and advances in medical technology are creating careers in healthcare administration, genetic counseling, and biotechnology innovation.

3. **Renewable Energy**: As sustainability becomes more critical, careers in solar and wind energy, green construction, and environmental engineering will see significant growth.

4. **Cybersecurity**: As digital transformation accelerates, cybersecurity professionals will be needed to protect data, networks, and systems from cyber threats.

5. **Robotics and Automation**: Robotics engineers and automation specialists will be crucial in developing systems to increase efficiency in manufacturing and other sectors.

6. **Remote Work Solutions**: With the rise of remote work, careers in virtual collaboration tools, remote team management, and remote technical support are expanding.

# Ask MrCareer
## *101 Common Questions About Careers and Their Answers*

By focusing on technology, sustainability, and healthcare, individuals can pursue career paths that are in demand and future-proof.

# Ask MrCareer
## *101 Common Questions About Careers and Their Answers*

# #72 - How will artificial intelligence impact job opportunities?

AI is reshaping industries and job opportunities, both creating new roles and transforming existing ones:

1. **Job Creation**: AI will generate new jobs in fields like AI development, machine learning, data analysis, and robotics. These require specialized skills and offer promising career paths.

2. **Automation of Routine Tasks**: AI will automate repetitive, manual tasks, such as data entry, customer service, and basic administrative functions, leading to job displacement in certain sectors.

3. **Increased Demand for AI-Related Roles**: As businesses integrate AI, demand will rise for roles in AI research, data science, and AI ethics. These fields require expertise in both technology and industry-specific applications.

4. **Augmented Work**: AI will enhance the work of professionals across industries. For example, AI tools can assist healthcare professionals in diagnosing conditions, improving efficiency, and reducing errors.

5. **Job Transformation**: AI will change how many jobs are done. Rather than replacing workers, AI may allow them to focus on higher-level tasks while automating routine functions.

The key to thriving in an AI-driven world is adapting by learning new skills, particularly in technology and data management.

# Ask MrCareer
*101 Common Questions About Careers and Their Answers*

## #73 - What industries are on the rise?

Several industries are seeing rapid growth due to technological advancements, demographic changes, and evolving consumer needs:

1. **Technology and AI**: The tech sector, particularly in AI, machine learning, cloud computing, and software development, continues to grow.

2. **Renewable Energy**: With the shift towards sustainability, renewable energy industries such as solar, wind, and electric vehicles are booming.

3. **Healthcare and Biotechnology**: As populations age and medical technology advances, healthcare, telemedicine, biotechnology, and pharmaceuticals are expanding rapidly.

4. **E-commerce and Online Services**: The growth of online shopping, digital marketing, and logistics is accelerating, driven by shifts in consumer behavior.

5. **Cybersecurity**: As cyber threats evolve, the cybersecurity industry is expanding, offering opportunities in IT security, data protection, and risk management.

By focusing on industries like technology, healthcare, and sustainability, individuals can position themselves for success in the future job market.

# Ask MrCareer
*101 Common Questions About Careers and Their Answers*

## #74 - How do I future-proof my career?

To future-proof your career, focus on adaptability, continuous learning, and staying ahead of industry trends:

1. **Learn New Skills**: Keep learning and developing new skills, especially those related to technology, data analytics, and problem-solving.

2. **Embrace Change**: Stay open to change and innovation in your industry. Being adaptable to new technologies and business models will make you invaluable.

3. **Networking**: Build a strong professional network. Relationships with industry leaders can provide insights into future trends and opportunities.

4. **Diversify Your Skills**: Learn to blend skills across different disciplines (e.g., combining tech skills with business acumen). Multi-disciplinary expertise is increasingly valuable.

5. **Stay Informed**: Follow industry news, attend webinars, and engage in professional development to understand emerging trends and technologies.

By staying informed, continuously learning, and embracing change, you can ensure long-term career success.

# Ask MrCareer
## 101 Common Questions About Careers and Their Answers

# #75 - What is the gig economy, and how does it affect careers?

The gig economy is a labor market characterized by short-term, flexible jobs often facilitated by online platforms:

1. **Freelancing and Contract Work**: Gig workers typically take on short-term contracts or freelance jobs, which offer flexibility but may lack stability and benefits like health insurance.

2. **Remote Opportunities**: The gig economy includes remote work, where workers can choose projects or clients across the globe.

3. **Entrepreneurial Opportunities**: The gig economy allows individuals to work as independent contractors, offering a way to build businesses around their skills.

4. **Income Variability**: Gig workers experience income uncertainty, as work may be inconsistent or fluctuating.

5. **Technology Platforms**: Platforms like Uber, Upwork, and Fiverr have enabled workers to access gigs in various fields, but these platforms can also create competition for jobs.

The gig economy offers flexibility and autonomy but comes with challenges like income instability and a lack of benefits. Understanding these dynamics is key for those considering gig work as a career path.

# Ask MrCareer
## *101 Common Questions About Careers and Their Answers*

## Specialized Careers

### #76 - What are the best careers in STEM?

STEM (Science, Technology, Engineering, and Mathematics) careers offer diverse opportunities across various fields. Some of the best careers in STEM, with high demand and lucrative potential, include:

1. **Software Developers and Engineers**: These professionals design and create software applications, websites, and mobile apps. With the growing tech industry, demand for software developers continues to rise.

2. **Data Scientists and Analysts**: Data scientists analyze complex data sets to uncover insights that help businesses make informed decisions. With the increasing reliance on big data, this field is rapidly expanding.

3. **Cybersecurity Experts**: As the number of cyberattacks increases, cybersecurity specialists are needed to protect sensitive data, networks, and systems from breaches.

4. **Biomedical Engineers**: These engineers work at the intersection of healthcare and engineering, designing medical devices and technologies that improve patient care.

5. **Environmental Engineers**: With a growing focus on sustainability, environmental engineers work on projects to protect the environment, including water treatment and pollution control.

# Ask MrCareer
## *101 Common Questions About Careers and Their Answers*

6. **Robotics Engineers**: Robotics professionals design and build robots that automate tasks in industries like manufacturing, healthcare, and logistics.

7. **Pharmacists and Pharmacologists**: These healthcare professionals play a critical role in medication management, developing new drugs, and improving health outcomes.

8. **Physicists and Chemists**: Research-driven roles in these fields often lead to breakthroughs in technology, energy, medicine, and manufacturing.

STEM careers are in high demand, and with the right education and skills, they can provide long-term job security and growth opportunities.

# Ask MrCareer
## *101 Common Questions About Careers and Their Answers*

# #77 - What are the highest-paying careers without a degree?

While many high-paying careers require a degree, there are several options where you can earn a great income without one:

1. **Commercial Pilot**: Pilots for non-commercial airlines, cargo companies, or charter services can earn significant salaries. While a degree isn't required, training, certifications, and flight hours are necessary.

2. **Air Traffic Controller**: Air traffic controllers guide aircraft during takeoff, landing, and while in flight, ensuring safety. The job requires certification and training but not a degree.

3. **Electricians**: Skilled electricians who work in residential, commercial, or industrial settings can earn high wages, especially with experience or specialization.

4. **Plumbers**: Similar to electricians, plumbers can earn a good income, particularly those who work as independent contractors or who specialize in certain areas of plumbing.

5. **Construction Managers**: Construction managers oversee building projects and construction teams. While a degree is beneficial, many enter the field through experience and training.

6. **Real Estate Brokers**: Real estate brokers can make substantial earnings by selling properties. Although a degree is not mandatory, licensing and industry knowledge are required.

7. **Firefighting Supervisors**: Firefighting positions, particularly in supervisory roles, offer competitive

# Ask MrCareer
## *101 Common Questions About Careers and Their Answers*

salaries. Specialized certifications and years of experience can elevate earning potential.

8. **Computer Support Specialists**: Professionals in IT support, such as network administrators or systems analysts, can earn high salaries with technical training and certifications.

9. **Wind Turbine Technicians**: With the rise of renewable energy, technicians who maintain wind turbines are in demand and can earn high wages with proper training.

10. **Truck Drivers**: Long-haul truck drivers, especially those with specialized trucking experience, can earn substantial salaries. Trucking requires licensing and specific certifications.

These careers offer solid financial potential, with many of them providing on-the-job training and certification programs rather than requiring a traditional four-year degree.

# Ask MrCareer
## *101 Common Questions About Careers and Their Answers*

## #78 - How do I enter creative industries like art or writing?

Entering creative industries like art or writing requires a combination of talent, skill development, networking, and determination:

1. **Build Your Portfolio**: For visual arts, a strong portfolio showcasing your best work is essential. For writers, maintain a collection of your written pieces, such as short stories, articles, or essays. A portfolio is key to demonstrating your capabilities to potential employers or clients.

2. **Develop Your Skills**: Continuously hone your craft by taking courses, attending workshops, and practicing regularly. Whether it's drawing, painting, or writing, constant improvement is vital to success in creative fields.

3. **Network and Collaborate**: Join creative communities, attend events like art exhibits or writing workshops, and connect with other professionals. Building relationships can lead to new opportunities.

4. **Use Social Media**: Platforms like Instagram, Behance, or LinkedIn can be used to showcase your work and gain visibility. For writers, blogs, Medium, or Wattpad offer great platforms to publish your work.

5. **Freelance or Intern**: Starting as a freelancer or an intern is a common path into creative industries. Look for internships or freelance jobs that allow you to gain experience and build a professional reputation.

# Ask MrCareer
## *101 Common Questions About Careers and Their Answers*

6. **Pitch Your Work**: When you're ready, submit your work to publications, galleries, or agents. Be persistent and professional when pitching your work to others.

7. **Stay Open to Feedback**: Creative industries are subjective, and not everyone will appreciate your work. Use criticism constructively to improve and grow.

Entering creative industries requires a balance of personal dedication, networking, and practical experience to make a successful career.

# Ask MrCareer
## *101 Common Questions About Careers and Their Answers*

## #79 - How can I succeed in healthcare careers?

Healthcare careers offer significant opportunities, but success in this field requires dedication and continuous learning. Here's how to succeed:

1. **Pursue Relevant Education and Training**: Depending on the role, completing the necessary certifications, degrees, or training programs is essential. Whether you're aiming for a doctor, nurse, technician, or administrator role, ensure you meet the educational requirements.

2. **Gain Practical Experience**: Internships, volunteer work, or part-time roles in healthcare settings allow you to gain firsthand experience and understand the working environment.

3. **Develop Soft Skills**: Healthcare professionals need strong communication, empathy, and teamwork skills. Developing these can improve patient care and your effectiveness on the job.

4. **Stay Updated**: Healthcare is an ever-evolving field with new technologies and medical advancements. Engage in continuous education to stay current on industry trends and techniques.

5. **Build a Network**: Establish relationships with professionals in your field through conferences, seminars, or online groups. Networking can lead to job opportunities and mentorship.

6. **Demonstrate Compassion and Patience**: Working in healthcare requires emotional resilience and the ability to interact with patients and their families compassionately.

# Ask MrCareer
## *101 Common Questions About Careers and Their Answers*

7. **Look for Specializations**: Specializing in a niche area of healthcare, such as pediatrics, anesthesiology, or radiology, can enhance your expertise and earning potential.

By committing to education, gaining experience, and maintaining compassion, you can succeed and make a meaningful impact in the healthcare field.

# Ask MrCareer
*101 Common Questions About Careers and Their Answers*

## #80 - What are career options for veterans?

Veterans bring a unique set of skills to the workforce, and many employers value their discipline and leadership experience. Career options for veterans include:

1. **Law Enforcement and Security**: Many veterans pursue careers in law enforcement, private security, or cybersecurity, leveraging their military training in security operations.

2. **Project Management**: Veterans' leadership and organizational skills are well-suited for project management roles in construction, IT, healthcare, and other industries.

3. **Healthcare**: Veterans can transition into healthcare careers as medical technicians, paramedics, nurses, or physicians, using their experience with military medical training.

4. **Technology**: With the right training, veterans can enter fields like software development, IT support, and network administration. Many technology companies offer programs tailored to veterans.

5. **Government and Civil Service**: Veterans may choose to work in federal or state government roles, as their military background makes them strong candidates for various public service positions.

6. **Entrepreneurship**: Many veterans start their own businesses. Entrepreneurial programs for veterans can help them navigate the challenges of starting and running a business.

# Ask MrCareer
## *101 Common Questions About Careers and Their Answers*

7. **Skilled Trades**: Veterans with hands-on skills can become electricians, plumbers, carpenters, or mechanics. Many trades offer training and certification programs that veterans can take advantage of.

Veterans have a wide range of career options, many of which directly build on their skills and experiences from military service.

# Ask MrCareer
### *101 Common Questions About Careers and Their Answers*

## Soft Skills and Career Success

### #81 - Why are communication skills critical for career success?

Communication skills are vital because they enable you to effectively convey ideas, collaborate with others, and build professional relationships. Here's why they matter:

1. **Effective Collaboration**: Clear communication allows teams to work together efficiently, ensuring everyone understands goals, expectations, and deadlines.

2. **Conflict Resolution**: Strong communication skills help in managing and resolving conflicts, both within teams and with clients or customers.

3. **Leadership**: Good leaders need to communicate vision, motivate their teams, and provide feedback. Effective communication fosters trust and respect.

4. **Career Advancement**: Professionals with excellent communication skills are often more visible and influential within an organization, making them prime candidates for promotions and leadership roles.

5. **Networking**: Being able to express yourself clearly is key to building relationships with peers, mentors, and potential employers.

6. **Client and Customer Relations**: Whether you're in sales, healthcare, or any customer-facing role, good communication skills are essential for building rapport and maintaining relationships.

# Ask MrCareer
## *101 Common Questions About Careers and Their Answers*

Developing strong communication skills can make you a more effective team member and a valuable asset to your organization.

# Ask MrCareer
*101 Common Questions About Careers and Their Answers*

## #82 - How do I develop leadership skills?

Leadership skills can be cultivated over time with intentional practice and learning. Here's how to develop them:

1. **Take Initiative**: Look for opportunities where you can take the lead, whether it's managing a project, mentoring a colleague, or organizing team activities.

2. **Learn from Other Leaders**: Observe and learn from other leaders. Pay attention to how they communicate, solve problems, and make decisions.

3. **Seek Feedback**: Ask for feedback on your leadership style from colleagues, mentors, or supervisors. Constructive criticism will help you improve.

4. **Improve Emotional Intelligence**: Leaders with high emotional intelligence can empathize with others, manage stress, and handle interpersonal relationships effectively.

5. **Develop Decision-Making Skills**: Leadership often involves making difficult decisions. Practice evaluating options, considering outcomes, and making informed choices.

6. **Lead by Example**: Demonstrate the values, work ethic, and behavior you expect from others. Your actions will inspire and motivate your team.

7. **Take Leadership Training**: Consider taking courses or attending seminars on leadership to gain new perspectives and tools.

Leadership is a skill that improves with experience and intentional development.

# Ask MrCareer
## *101 Common Questions About Careers and Their Answers*

# #83 - What are the most valuable interpersonal skills for the workplace?

Interpersonal skills are essential for building relationships, collaborating effectively, and contributing to a positive work environment. Some of the most valuable interpersonal skills include:

1. **Communication**: The ability to express ideas clearly and listen actively to others is key to effective collaboration.

2. **Empathy**: Understanding and recognizing the emotions and needs of others helps foster a supportive and respectful environment.

3. **Teamwork**: The ability to work well with others toward a common goal is essential for success in almost every workplace.

4. **Conflict Resolution**: Being able to mediate disputes, find common ground, and resolve conflicts in a constructive manner is crucial.

5. **Adaptability**: Being flexible and willing to work with diverse people and in changing environments helps teams stay effective.

6. **Negotiation**: Strong negotiators can manage disagreements and find mutually beneficial solutions while maintaining professional relationships.

7. **Trustworthiness**: Building trust with colleagues and clients is fundamental to any successful working relationship.

Having strong interpersonal skills will make you more effective in your role and increase your chances of career success.

# Ask MrCareer
## *101 Common Questions About Careers and Their Answers*

## #84 - How do I handle conflict in the workplace?

Handling conflict effectively is crucial for maintaining a positive and productive work environment. Here are strategies to resolve workplace conflict:

1. **Stay Calm and Objective**: Avoid reacting emotionally and focus on the facts of the situation. Take time to listen to both sides.

2. **Communicate Openly**: Encourage open dialogue between the parties involved. Be respectful and listen actively to their perspectives.

3. **Seek Common Ground**: Try to understand the underlying issues and identify areas where compromise is possible.

4. **Involve a Mediator**: If direct communication doesn't work, consider involving a neutral third party, such as a supervisor or HR professional.

5. **Focus on Solutions**: Shift the conversation from blame to problem-solving. Work together to find a resolution that benefits everyone.

6. **Set Boundaries**: In ongoing conflicts, set clear boundaries and agree on how to move forward constructively.

7. **Document the Situation**: If necessary, keep records of the conflict and any resolutions or agreements to protect yourself or the organization.

By managing conflicts professionally, you can help maintain a positive workplace culture.

# Ask MrCareer
## *101 Common Questions About Careers and Their Answers*

# #85 - How do I build confidence in my abilities?

Building confidence takes time and consistent effort. Here's how you can strengthen your self-assurance:

1. **Set Achievable Goals**: Start with small, manageable goals that allow you to experience success. Gradually increase the difficulty as your confidence grows.

2. **Reflect on Your Strengths**: Regularly remind yourself of your accomplishments and the skills that make you unique and valuable.

3. **Practice Self-Affirmation**: Use positive self-talk to challenge self-doubt and reinforce your belief in your abilities.

4. **Seek Feedback**: Constructive feedback from colleagues, mentors, or supervisors can boost confidence by helping you recognize areas for improvement.

5. **Prepare Thoroughly**: Being well-prepared for tasks and challenges increases your confidence in your ability to succeed.

6. **Learn from Mistakes**: Accept that mistakes are part of the learning process. Use them as opportunities for growth rather than setbacks.

7. **Visualize Success**: Imagine yourself succeeding in various scenarios. Visualization can help reinforce your belief in your ability to succeed.

Building confidence is a gradual process that requires patience, self-compassion, and a proactive approach to personal growth.

# Ask MrCareer
*101 Common Questions About Careers and Their Answers*

## Miscellaneous Topics

### #86 - What are the best tools for career planning?

Career planning involves assessing your current position, setting future goals, and creating a roadmap to achieve them. Some of the best tools for career planning include:

1. **Self-Assessment Tools**: Tools like StrengthsFinder, Myers-Briggs Type Indicator (MBTI), or the Holland Code can help you understand your skills, personality, and interests, which can guide your career choices.

2. **Career Mapping Software**: Tools like MindTools or CareerOneStop provide templates and guidance for mapping out potential career paths and setting clear objectives.

3. **Goal Setting Tools**: Applications such as Trello, Todoist, or Google Calendar help you organize your short-term and long-term goals and track your progress.

4. **Networking Platforms**: LinkedIn is a powerful tool for networking, job searching, and staying informed about industry trends.

5. **Online Courses and Certifications**: Websites like Coursera, LinkedIn Learning, and edX offer opportunities to gain new skills, which can be valuable for career advancement.

6. **Mentorship Programs**: Mentorship helps you receive guidance from someone more experienced in your field. Many organizations and career coaching platforms provide structured mentorship programs.

# Ask MrCareer
## *101 Common Questions About Careers and Their Answers*

Using a combination of these tools can give you a well-rounded approach to planning and advancing your career.

# Ask MrCareer
## *101 Common Questions About Careers and Their Answers*

## #87 - How do I write an effective resume?

An effective resume should highlight your skills, experience, and accomplishments in a clear and concise manner. Here are steps to create one:

1. **Contact Information**: Start with your name, phone number, email address, and location (city, state).

2. **Professional Summary or Objective**: Write a brief statement (2-3 sentences) summarizing your qualifications and what you aim to achieve in your next role.

3. **Skills**: List both hard and soft skills relevant to the job you're applying for. Use bullet points for easy reading.

4. **Work Experience**: Include your most relevant job experiences, starting with the most recent. For each role, list key responsibilities and achievements. Quantify accomplishments when possible (e.g., "Increased sales by 20%").

5. **Education**: Include your degree(s), the school(s) you attended, and graduation dates. If you're early in your career, place this section above work experience.

6. **Certifications and Training**: List any relevant certifications or specialized training.

7. **Volunteer Work or Extracurricular Activities**: Include if relevant to the role or industry, showcasing leadership or teamwork abilities.

8. **Tailoring**: Customize your resume for each job you apply to, highlighting the skills and experience that align with the job description.

# Ask MrCareer
## *101 Common Questions About Careers and Their Answers*

A strong resume should be concise (1-2 pages), free of errors, and formatted clearly for easy reading.

# Ask MrCareer
## *101 Common Questions About Careers and Their Answers*

# #88 - What is the importance of mentorship in a career?

Mentorship plays a vital role in career growth and personal development. Here's why it's important:

1. **Guidance and Wisdom**: A mentor provides invaluable advice based on their own experiences, helping you navigate challenges and avoid common mistakes.

2. **Skill Development**: Mentors can help you identify your strengths and areas for improvement, offering feedback to refine your skills.

3. **Networking Opportunities**: Mentors often introduce you to their professional network, opening doors for career opportunities and collaborations.

4. **Emotional Support**: Mentors can be a source of encouragement during difficult times, providing motivation and confidence to keep progressing.

5. **Goal Setting**: A mentor helps you set realistic, achievable goals and holds you accountable, ensuring you stay on track in your career journey.

6. **Broadening Perspective**: By having a mentor, you gain new insights, ideas, and ways of thinking that expand your view of the industry or field you're in.

Mentorship can significantly accelerate your professional growth and provide long-term career benefits.

# Ask MrCareer
## *101 Common Questions About Careers and Their Answers*

## #89 - How do internships help in career building?

Internships are a valuable way to gain hands-on experience, develop skills, and build professional networks. Here's how they contribute to career building:

1. **Real-World Experience**: Internships allow you to apply what you've learned in school to actual workplace scenarios, which helps build your confidence and expertise.

2. **Skill Development**: Internships help you develop both technical and soft skills (e.g., communication, teamwork) that are crucial for your career.

3. **Networking**: Working in a professional setting provides the opportunity to meet and form relationships with industry professionals who can offer valuable advice and job opportunities.

4. **Exploring Career Paths**: Internships allow you to test different roles within your field, helping you decide which direction to take your career in.

5. **Resume Building**: Internships enhance your resume by showing potential employers that you have practical experience and initiative.

6. **Job Opportunities**: Many companies offer full-time positions to successful interns, providing a smooth transition from education to employment.

Internships can serve as a stepping stone, offering practical experience and connections that can lead to a permanent role.

# Ask MrCareer
*101 Common Questions About Careers and Their Answers*

## #90 - Should I work abroad to grow my career?

Working abroad can offer many benefits for career growth. Consider the following advantages:

1. **Global Experience**: International experience can broaden your perspective, helping you understand diverse cultures and markets, which is highly valued in globalized industries.

2. **Networking**: Living and working abroad exposes you to new professional networks, which could lead to opportunities in international companies or industries.

3. **Skill Enhancement**: You may gain unique skills that are in demand globally, such as proficiency in foreign languages or understanding international business practices.

4. **Career Advancement**: Many multinational companies value employees with international experience because it demonstrates adaptability, cultural competence, and a global mindset.

5. **Personal Growth**: Working abroad challenges you to step out of your comfort zone, which can foster resilience, independence, and personal development.

6. **Higher Earning Potential**: Some countries offer higher salaries or attractive benefits for skilled workers, especially in industries like tech, finance, or engineering.

However, it's important to consider the challenges, such as adjusting to a new culture, managing work-life balance, and navigating legal or visa requirements.

# Ask MrCareer
## *101 Common Questions About Careers and Their Answers*

# Job Search and Interviews

## #91 - How do I prepare for an interview?

Preparation is key to making a great impression in an interview. Follow these steps:

1. **Research the Company**: Learn about the company's mission, values, products/services, culture, and recent news. Understand how your skills align with their needs.

2. **Understand the Job Description**: Review the job requirements and responsibilities, and think about how your experience fits.

3. **Practice Common Interview Questions**: Prepare answers to common questions like "Tell me about yourself," "What are your strengths and weaknesses?" and "Why do you want to work here?"

4. **Prepare Questions to Ask**: Have a list of thoughtful questions for the interviewer, such as "What does success look like in this role?" or "How do you define the company culture?"

5. **Plan Your Attire**: Dress appropriately for the company culture and the position you're applying for.

6. **Practice Body Language**: Pay attention to your posture, eye contact, and handshake. Positive body language conveys confidence and professionalism.

7. **Bring Necessary Materials**: Bring copies of your resume, portfolio (if relevant), and any other materials the interviewer may need.

# Ask MrCareer
## *101 Common Questions About Careers and Their Answers*

8. **Be Prepared to Discuss Salary Expectations**: Know your worth and be ready to discuss salary and benefits if the topic arises.

Preparing well helps you feel confident and enables you to make a strong impression on your potential employer.

# Ask MrCareer
## *101 Common Questions About Careers and Their Answers*

## #92 - What are the best ways to find a job?

Finding a job requires a mix of strategies. Here are some of the best ways:

1. **Online Job Portals**: Websites like LinkedIn, Indeed, Glassdoor, and ZipRecruiter list job openings and allow you to apply directly.

2. **Networking**: Networking with colleagues, mentors, and industry professionals can lead to job leads and referrals. Attend industry events or engage in online communities.

3. **Company Websites**: Research companies you're interested in and apply directly through their career pages.

4. **Recruitment Agencies**: Many industries have specialized recruitment agencies that can match you with job opportunities based on your skills and experience.

5. **Social Media**: Use LinkedIn to connect with recruiters, join relevant groups, and follow companies that align with your career goals.

6. **Job Fairs**: Attend job fairs, either in person or virtually, where you can meet employers and learn about job opportunities.

7. **Cold Outreach**: Reach out to companies that interest you, even if they're not currently hiring. Express your interest and inquire about future openings.

By using multiple job search methods, you increase your chances of finding a suitable position.

# Ask MrCareer
*101 Common Questions About Careers and Their Answers*

## #93 - How do I negotiate my salary?

Negotiating your salary requires preparation and confidence. Here's how to do it:

1. **Do Your Research**: Find out the average salary for the role in your location and industry by using websites like Glassdoor, Payscale, or the Bureau of Labor Statistics.

2. **Know Your Worth**: Assess your skills, experience, and achievements to understand your value to the company.

3. **Wait for the Right Moment**: Ideally, wait until you've been offered the job before discussing salary. If you're negotiating for a raise, choose a time when your recent accomplishments are fresh.

4. **Frame the Conversation Positively**: Approach the discussion from a perspective of mutual benefit. For example, you might say, "I'm excited about the opportunity and based on my research, I believe a salary of $X is appropriate for my skills and experience."

5. **Consider Benefits and Perks**: If the salary offer is non-negotiable, see if there are other benefits, like extra vacation time, flexible work hours, or a signing bonus, that can be negotiated.

6. **Be Prepared to Justify**: Be ready to explain why you believe you deserve the salary you're asking for based on your qualifications and experience.

7. **Stay Professional**: Be respectful, and if the employer can't meet your salary request, discuss alternative solutions that might work for both sides.

Salary negotiation is a key skill that ensures you're compensated fairly for your work.

# Ask MrCareer
## *101 Common Questions About Careers and Their Answers*

# #94 - What questions should I ask in an interview?

Asking insightful questions during an interview shows you're engaged and interested. Consider asking:

1. **About the Role**: "What does a typical day look like for someone in this position?"

2. **About Expectations**: "What are the immediate challenges that need to be addressed in this role?"

3. **About the Team**: "Can you describe the team I'll be working with and how they collaborate?"

4. **About Success Metrics**: "How do you measure success for this role?"

5. **About Growth Opportunities**: "What opportunities are available for professional development and growth within the company?"

6. **About Company Culture**: "How would you describe the company culture, and how does this team contribute to it?"

7. **About Next Steps**: "What are the next steps in the hiring process, and when can I expect to hear back?"

Asking questions gives you insight into the role and demonstrates your genuine interest in the company.

# Ask MrCareer
## *101 Common Questions About Careers and Their Answers*

## #95 - How do I deal with job rejections?

Job rejections can be discouraging, but there are ways to cope and grow from the experience:

1. **Allow Yourself to Feel Disappointed**: It's natural to feel upset, so allow yourself time to process the rejection.

2. **Ask for Feedback**: Politely ask the interviewer for feedback on why you weren't selected. Use this information to improve for future interviews.

3. **Learn and Improve**: Reflect on the experience to identify areas for improvement in your resume, interview performance, or skills.

4. **Stay Positive**: Reframe the rejection as an opportunity for growth, and trust that the right job will come along.

5. **Keep Applying**: Don't be discouraged by one rejection. Keep applying and expanding your job search to increase your chances of success.

Remember, rejection is often a part of the job search process, and each setback brings you closer to finding the right role.

# Ask MrCareer
## 101 Common Questions About Careers and Their Answers

# Retirement and Legacy

## #96 - How do I plan for retirement in my career?

Planning for retirement is a critical part of long-term career success. Here's how to approach it:

1. **Start Early**: Begin planning as soon as possible to give your savings time to grow. The earlier you start, the more you'll benefit from compound interest.

2. **Evaluate Your Retirement Needs**: Estimate how much money you'll need for retirement by considering your desired lifestyle, healthcare costs, housing, and any debts or obligations you may have.

3. **Contribute to Retirement Accounts**: Take advantage of retirement savings plans like 401(k)s, IRAs, or pension plans. Contribute regularly and aim to max out contributions if possible, especially if your employer offers matching funds.

4. **Diversify Investments**: Invest in a variety of assets (stocks, bonds, real estate) to reduce risk and ensure steady growth. Consult with a financial advisor for tailored advice.

5. **Create a Retirement Budget**: Start by tracking your expenses to understand how much you'll need in retirement. Then, make adjustments to save more if necessary.

6. **Plan for Healthcare**: Consider healthcare costs in retirement, including premiums for insurance and out-of-pocket expenses. Look into Medicare or private health insurance options.

# Ask MrCareer
## *101 Common Questions About Careers and Their Answers*

7. **Reevaluate Regularly**: As your career progresses and your financial situation changes, review and adjust your retirement plan to stay on track.

8. **Establish an Estate Plan**: Make sure your will, trusts, and power of attorney documents are in place to manage your assets when you're no longer able to do so.

Taking these steps ensures that you can transition into retirement comfortably and securely.

# Ask MrCareer
## *101 Common Questions About Careers and Their Answers*

## #97 - What is the legacy I want to leave in my career?

The legacy you leave in your career is the lasting impact you have on your profession, colleagues, and community. Consider the following to define your legacy:

1. **Career Contributions**: Reflect on the value you've added to your industry, company, or organization. This might include innovations, projects, or initiatives that made a difference.

2. **Mentorship and Influence**: Think about how you've helped shape the careers of others through mentorship or by setting a positive example. Inspiring others to grow professionally is a powerful legacy.

3. **Ethics and Values**: Consider the principles you've adhered to in your career, such as honesty, integrity, and fairness. A legacy built on strong ethical values can be an enduring influence.

4. **Knowledge Transfer**: Passing on your expertise through writing, training, or teaching can be part of your career legacy. Sharing your knowledge with others ensures that your contributions live on.

5. **Community Impact**: If you've been involved in professional organizations, community service, or philanthropy, those contributions can also form a part of your legacy.

6. **Personal Growth and Fulfillment**: The legacy you leave can also be about the personal satisfaction and fulfillment you've derived from your work, and how that inspires others to pursue meaningful careers.

# Ask MrCareer
## *101 Common Questions About Careers and Their Answers*

Your legacy is the result of the cumulative impact you've had over the course of your career.

# Ask MrCareer
## *101 Common Questions About Careers and Their Answers*

# #98 - How do I stay active after retiring from my career?

Staying active after retirement is crucial for maintaining both physical and mental well-being. Here are ways to stay active:

1. **Exercise Regularly**: Engage in activities like walking, swimming, yoga, or cycling. Physical exercise is essential for maintaining health, mobility, and vitality.

2. **Take Up New Hobbies**: Retirement gives you time to explore interests you didn't have time for during your career. Whether it's painting, gardening, or learning a musical instrument, new hobbies can keep you engaged and fulfilled.

3. **Volunteer**: Volunteering can provide a sense of purpose and community. Consider helping out at local charities, schools, or senior centers.

4. **Part-Time Work or Consulting**: If you enjoy working but want to reduce your hours, consider part-time work or offering consulting services in your area of expertise. This keeps your skills sharp and helps you stay connected to your industry.

5. **Social Engagement**: Stay active in social circles by joining clubs, attending meetups, or maintaining close relationships with family and friends. Social interactions are vital for mental health.

6. **Lifelong Learning**: Continue learning through online courses, reading, or taking up new educational pursuits. This can stimulate your brain and provide a sense of accomplishment.

# Ask MrCareer
## *101 Common Questions About Careers and Their Answers*

7. **Travel**: If finances and health allow, consider traveling as a way to stay engaged with the world, experience new cultures, and keep your sense of adventure alive.

Staying physically and mentally active after retirement can help you live a long, fulfilling, and healthy post-career life.

# Ask MrCareer
## *101 Common Questions About Careers and Their Answers*

## #99 - What are second-act careers?

A second-act career refers to pursuing a new career or professional endeavor after retiring or transitioning from a previous one. Here's what it entails:

1. **New Beginnings**: A second-act career is often a chance to do something different from your first career—perhaps in a completely different field or a related passion. It allows you to start fresh, leveraging the experience and skills gained from your previous work.

2. **Pursuing Passions**: Many people transition into careers they are passionate about but couldn't pursue earlier due to financial or personal constraints. Examples include turning a hobby like writing, art, or cooking into a business.

3. **Flexible Work**: Second-act careers often allow for more flexibility in terms of work hours and responsibilities. For instance, consulting, freelance work, or part-time roles can provide a better work-life balance.

4. **Philanthropy or Nonprofits**: Some retirees choose a second act focused on giving back, working in the nonprofit sector, or starting charitable organizations.

5. **Skill Utilization**: Often, a second-act career allows individuals to continue using their professional skills in a new context, such as mentoring, teaching, or consulting, without the pressure of a full-time job.

6. **Entrepreneurship**: Many people take the opportunity in their second act to start their own businesses, leveraging their experience and resources to pursue new entrepreneurial ventures.

# Ask MrCareer
## *101 Common Questions About Careers and Their Answers*

A second-act career is an opportunity to redefine your professional life after retirement, providing new challenges and growth.

# Ask MrCareer
## *101 Common Questions About Careers and Their Answers*

# #100 - How do I pass on career wisdom to the next generation?

Passing on your career wisdom is essential for nurturing the growth of the next generation of professionals. Here are ways to do so:

1. **Mentoring**: Act as a mentor to younger professionals, sharing your experiences, offering advice, and providing guidance in their career paths. Help them navigate challenges and setbacks.

2. **Creating Educational Content**: Write books, blogs, or articles on career-related topics to pass on your knowledge to a broader audience.

3. **Offering Internships**: Provide internship opportunities to students or recent graduates, helping them gain hands-on experience in the field and learn from your expertise.

4. **Leading by Example**: Set a strong example through your work ethic, professionalism, and attitude. Demonstrating how to handle success and failure can offer valuable life lessons.

5. **Speaking Engagements**: Share your career journey and insights through speaking engagements at universities, conferences, or industry events.

6. **Volunteer Coaching**: Offer to coach or provide career advice in community centers, schools, or professional organizations. Help individuals explore career options and set goals.

By actively engaging with younger generations, you can provide invaluable guidance that helps them build successful careers.

# Ask MrCareer
## *101 Common Questions About Careers and Their Answers*

# Final Question

## #101 - How do I define success in my career?

Defining success in your career is a deeply personal process that depends on your values, goals, and aspirations. Here are some ways to define success:

1. **Personal Fulfillment**: Success could mean pursuing a career that aligns with your passions and values, finding joy in your work, and achieving a sense of purpose.

2. **Professional Achievements**: For some, success may be defined by professional milestones, such as promotions, recognition, or the completion of major projects.

3. **Work-Life Balance**: Success can be about achieving a balance between your career and personal life, ensuring you have time for family, hobbies, and self-care.

4. **Financial Stability**: For many, success includes achieving financial security and independence through career earnings, savings, and investments.

5. **Impact on Others**: Success might also involve making a positive impact on your team, company, or industry, such as through mentoring, leadership, or contributing to meaningful change.

6. **Legacy**: Success may also be about the legacy you leave behind, whether through the relationships you've built, the knowledge you've shared, or the positive mark you've made on the world.

Ultimately, career success is subjective and should reflect what you value most in your professional and personal life.

# Ask MrCareer
## *101 Common Questions About Careers and Their Answers*

# Final Thoughts

Your career is more than just a job or a series of roles—it's a journey of growth, discovery, and purpose. Throughout this book, *Ask MrCareer: 101 Common Questions About Careers and Their Answers*, we have explored the many facets of building, advancing, and redefining a career. From the initial steps of choosing the right path to navigating challenges, seizing opportunities, and planning for the future, the answers provided here are meant to empower and guide you toward a fulfilling professional life.

Every question addressed in this book is rooted in the real-life experiences and challenges people face as they navigate their careers. Whether you are just starting out, considering a major change, or planning for retirement, these insights aim to inspire confidence and provide practical tools to help you take charge of your career trajectory. The lessons shared are not only about finding success but also about aligning your professional aspirations with your values, passions, and long-term goals.

One of the key takeaways from this journey is the importance of adaptability. In a world of constant change, flexibility and a willingness to learn are invaluable assets. Your career path may not always follow a straight line, but each twist and turn presents an opportunity for growth and reinvention. Embracing these moments can lead to unexpected successes and greater personal fulfillment.

As you move forward, remember that your career is a reflection of your unique talents, ambitions, and resilience. Take time to reflect on what truly matters to you, stay curious about new possibilities, and never stop striving for improvement. Whether it's through cultivating new skills, networking, or finding a better work-life balance, the steps you take today can shape a brighter future.

# Ask MrCareer
## *101 Common Questions About Careers and Their Answers*

This book is just the beginning. The answers here are a foundation, but the journey is yours to complete. As you embark on your next chapter, trust in your ability to grow, adapt, and succeed. The tools and strategies you've gained from *Ask MrCareer* are here to support you every step of the way. Here's to your continued success and fulfillment in your career journey!

*"Unlock even more powerful tools for success with the Smart Dozen series! Visit [SmartDozen.com](http://SmartDozen.com) to browse our full collection of books, each tailored to help you thrive in a different area of life. Your journey to success doesn't end here!"*

# Ask MrCareer
*101 Common Questions About Careers and Their Answers*

# Notes

# Ask MrCareer
*101 Common Questions About Careers and Their Answers*

# Notes

**Ask MrCareer**
*101 Common Questions About Careers and Their Answers*

# Notes

**Ask MrCareer**
*101 Common Questions About Careers and Their Answers*

# Notes

# Ask MrCareer
*101 Common Questions About Careers and Their Answers*

# Notes